EIGHTEENTH CENTURY SHAKESPEARE
No. 6

General Editor : Professor Arthur Freeman, Boston University

AN ESSAY
UPON ENGLISH TRAGEDY

Together with

AN ATTEMPTE
To Rescue that Aunciente, English Poet, and Play-Wrighte

Maister WILLIAUME SHAKESPERE

A complete list of titles in this series
is included at the end of this volume.

AN ESSAY

UPON

ENGLISH TRAGEDY

with

Remarks upon the Abbe de Blanc's Observations on
the English Stage

BY

WILLIAM GUTHRIE

TOGETHER WITH

AN ATTEMPTE

TO RESCUE THAT

Aunciente English Poet And Play-Wrighte

Maister WILLIAUME SHAKESPERE

From the Maney Errours, faulsely charged on him,
by Certaine New-fangled Wittes

BY

JOHN HOLT

FRANK CASS & CO. LTD.
1971

Published by
FRANK CASS AND COMPANY LIMITED
67 Great Russell Street, London WC1B 3BT

New preface Copyright © 1971 Arthur Freeman

An Essay Upon English Tragedy

First edition   1747

Reprint of First edition
with a new preface   1971

An Attempte to Rescue Shakespere

First edition   1749

Reprint of First edition
with a new preface   1971

ISBN 0 7146 2524 8

Printed in Great Britain by Clarke, Doble & Brendon Ltd.
Plymouth and London

PREFACE

An Essay upon English Tragedy

William Guthrie's undated *Essay* has been variously assigned to the years 1747 (Jaggard; *CBEL*, I, 593, and followers) and 1757 (*DNB*; *CBEL*, II, 887, and *BMC*); additionally, *CBEL* cites an edition, unseen by me and very likely a ghost, of '1749'. T. Waller also published Dr. Dodd's *Beauties of Shakespeare* in 1752 (cf. Plomer, p. 254) and Whalley's *Enquiry* (1748), but little is known of him. However, the remarks of Abbé Jean Bernard LeBlanc (whom Guthrie's title-page calls 'De Blanc') appear first in the Abbé's *Lettres d'un François*, published anonymously at 'La Haye' [Paris: *teste* Quérard] in 1745, and were first translated into English in 1747 (two eds., Dublin and London). In view of the stir they created, and Guthrie's insistence on considering the questions raised by them at the end of his short essay, the date of 1747 seems most probable.

Guthrie's *Essay* has long enjoyed an underground reputation for its terse sagacity. One might compare the trenchant, if censorious, description of *The Merry Wives of Windsor* here, with the unequivocal approbation offered in Gildon's *Life of Betterton* less than forty years before. On the other side of the ledger, we may be surprised to discover that 'the other genius of English Tragedy' is 'the author of *The Orphan*', Thomas Otway, although Otway's popularity at this time was enormous.

Two issues exist: the earlier collates $A^7B^8D^2$ [British Museum 1484.dd.39], the first word on $D1^r$ 'ciently'; the corrected issue $A^7B^8C^2$, rendering the first word on $C1^r$ rightly as 'ently', and regularizing the collation. No other changes have been observed; the press-number '3' occurs in both at p. 24; and apparently [A8] has been cancelled in all copies I have seen, with no discontinuity of catchwords.

Guthrie is the subject of a short biography in *DNB*, and as a friend of Dr. Johnson appears occasionally in the *Life*, as well as in Nichols' *Anecdotes* and *Illustrations*. The present reprint is prepared from a copy of the corrected issue in the Birmingham Public Library, compared with British Museum 11795.e.34, and the Harvard and Boston Public Library copies.

September, 1970   A. F.

PREFACE

An Attempte

Despite its monstrously eccentric title, *An Attempte* is quite simply a short textual and critical commentary upon *The Tempest*, one of many pamphlets provoked by the appearance of Warburton's pontifical edition in 1747. It contains, as Furness points out, the first serious attempt to establish a date of composition for *The Tempest*, a problem which remained one of the thorniest in Shakespeare scholarship for nearly a century; it offers suggested emendations, including a fairly popular solution to the 'most busy least' crux in III. i., as well as explication and explanatory comparison; it is in fact also, apparently, the earliest book devoted exclusively to that single play.

But *An Attempte* has scarcely commanded a great deal of attention. Its author pleads that if he is 'mistaken' in his opinions, ''tis presumed his Love and Esteem for *Shakespear*, will procure his Pardon for this Essay, and his future Silence, atone for his present Error'. Perhaps he himself admitted defeat; indeed, it appears that the edition, 'printed for the Author, and sold by Messieurs Manby and Cox', remained inexhausted when in 1750 it reappeared—this time 'for Manby and Cox' alone—with a simpler cancel title, and conjugate, if half-hearted proposals for a whole new edition of Shakespeare to be prepared by the still-anonymous commentator. Nothing came of the latter project, and little weight was allowed the critical or textual remarks by subsequent editors. Capell, Johnson, and Steevens ignore them altogether, and while Malone gives *An Attempte* a contemptuous citation or two in 1790, it does not appear among Malone's 'authorities' in his working copy, the great annotated Capell (1760–68) preserved in the British Museum. The essay has not been reprinted, and is never even mentioned by Chambers, Ralli, or by Nichol Smith.

A mystery surrounds the authorship of *An Attempte*, moreover. The name 'Holt' is often found, in early MS., on the title-page above or alongside 'By a Gentleman formerly of Grey's Inn'. The earliest printed allusion to the pamphlet, as far as I know, appears in the enlarged third Johnson–Steevens edition of the *Works* (1785), I, 263, where it is ascribed to '[Mr. Holt]'; and in general in that 1785 list of 'separate books' about Shakespeare, first names *are* given—presumably when known. Likewise in Malone's edition (1790), Malone's *Account of the . . . Tempest* (1808–09, and Boswell–Malone (1821), in the earliest separate bibliography of Shakespeare (by John Wilson, 1827), in the Dent sale (1827), and in the Douce Catalogue (1840) it is always just 'Holt'. By about 1860, however, the identification has become expanded to 'John Holt'—as subsequently in Jaggard, Halkett and Laing, the *BMC*, etc.—for no reason I can ascertain. The only possible 'John Holt' listed by Foster in his *Register* of Gray's Inn admissions matriculated at Peterhouse in 1709, married the Duke of Wharton's sister in 1723, stood unsuccessfully for Knight of the Shire (Suffolk) in 1727, and was buried in the same year at Redgrave (see Venn, and the Suffolk Poll-

Book printed at Ipswich, 1727). There simply is no other Gray's Inn John Holt in the *Register* or *Pension Book* whose dates fit at all, nor, curiously, is there any copy of the pamphlet in Gray's Inn library. No record of book or author may be found in the Gentleman's Magazine, the Annual Review, or in Nichols. Other Holts, of course, are listed by Foster, but I cannot pin any of them down to the book; might the whole appellation be some kind of play on the title-page of Edwards' *Canons of Criticism*? 'Holt' has further been confused with Holt White, an amateur Shakespearean of the latter part of the century, by the first Cambridge editors; and a final, maddening note is the *BMC*'s 'by [J. H.]' for the 1750 issue, whereas no initials appear in any copy seen by me.

The present reprint is prepared from a copy of the first edition in the Birmingham Public Library, compared with examples in the British Museum (2), Boston Public Library, and Harvard. It collates A–M⁴ [M4 blank]. In the 1750 reissue [A1] is cancelled and replaced by quarter-sheet [ ]². We reproduce as an appendix the 1750 [ ]² (proposals and title-page) from the British Museum copy (80.d.29). [ ]1ʳ is blank.

August, 1970   A. F.

A N

ESSAY

UPON

ENGLISH TRAGEDY.

WITH

REMARKS upon the Abbe de *Blanc*'s
Observations on the ENGLISH STAGE.

By WILLIAM GUTHRIE, *Esq;*

Printed for T. WALLER, at the *Crown* and *Mitre*,
opposite *Fetter-lane*, in *Fleet-street*.

A N
E S S A Y
UPON
ENGLISH TRAGEDY.

T is little above a century since the drama was critically confidered. The affemblies formed under the patronage of cardinal Richelieu, and which afterwards improved into an academy, gave encouragement to Corneille. His were the firft regular plays, which, perhaps, France, Spain, or Italy, had ever feen fince the days of the antients. He was fucceeded by Racine ; and to the firft of thefe poets, the French gave the epithet of SUBLIME ; to the latter, that of NATURAL.

THE truth is, nothing can be better conceived than is the diftrefs of Corneille's Cid ; and Racine wrote feveral tragedies, of which our middling rate of Englifh Poets need not to be afhamed.

BUT the arts to which thofe two poets owed their extravagant reputation all over Europe, have been but little attended to ; and ftill continue to debauch, to delude, and to enervate genius. Let us endeavour, if we can, to ftrip off the impofing ornaments, and to correct the illufive glare.

OF that affembly I have already mentioned, fome members were mere poets, and critics ; others, though the fmaller number, were men of fenfe and knowledge of the world. Thefe laft

were

were entrufted with the fecret of their government's noble defign ; that of eftablifhing an uni-
verfal empire, in arts as well as in arms. They
therefore availed themfelves of the bright fide of
their poets merits. Critical learning had, fome
time before, taken its flight to this fide of the
Alps, and fettled in France ; and their two favourite poets were conceived to have a fufficiency of
elevation, when illuftrated by the chafte conduct
of their plays, to fet them up as the ftandards of
the modern drama ; and, in fome refpects, as fuperior to the antients themfelves.

THIS defign was actually carried into execution, by a profufion of ingenious criticifms, diſſertations, and effays, concerning the conduct of
the drama ; efpecially with regard to the unities
of time, place, and character. As the French
were authors of thofe performances, the univerfa-
lity of their language foon poured them into
tranflations, all over the polite parts of Europe ; and
the ignorant, degenerated, though witty, court of
Charles II. encouraged the French drama, almoft
to idolatry. The fair, the noble, the witty, and
the gay, clubbed their endeavours to make Corneille and Racine fpeak Englifh ; nor could even
the poor figure, which thofe authors made in an
Englifh tranflation, cure the ridiculous paffion.
Pride, or prepoffeffion, continued the delufion
which affectation had begun, 'till, with Otway,
genius fled, and poetry fucceeded.

PARDON this diftinction, which has but too
fuccefsfully been abolifhed by the French, who
never yet produced a poet with one fpark of that
real fire which animates a true dramatic genius.
When preft with this defect they poorly labour to
cover it, by the pretence of their attachment to
the rules of the ftage. But it is mere feeblenefs.
They

They, however, made admirable use of their critical learning ; and wrote, or talked, down the invention of Lopez de Vega, and the vein of Calderon, the Spanish poets, with whom the first patrons of their reformed stage could not be unacquainted ; but they dreaded a comparison of genius, and gave the subject such a turn, as that no such comparison could be admitted.

I HAVE hitherto confined myself to speak of tragedy, and have avoided all mention of the English stage. My reason for the first is, because I think Moliere is, in comedy, a true genius. But we here see the management of the French. Where no real genius appears, (as they have none in tragedy,) the strict adherence to the rules and purity of the drama covers all defects. But where (as in Moliere) there is great merit, the offences against rules are pardoned ; and Moliere is admitted to stand at the head of French comedy, notwithstanding all his lameness in plots, and other defects in his plays.

As to my not mentioning the English stage ; we cannot accuse the French of having done it the injustice which they have done to the Spanish and Italian theatres. Their first reformers, and best authors, appear to have been, not only utterly unacquainted with our language, but ignorant that we had any stage excepting what precariously subsisted upon translations from them. We will now, however, consider the mighty merit of French critical learning, when applied to the English stage.

THE rules of the drama are really no discoveries ; they are not inventions of which the French can boast. Even the antients themselves owed them to nature, and to their good sense. Their poets gave the examples ; and, from those examples

amples, their critics formed rules. This is a fact eafily to be proved. Thus dramatic poetry ſtands upon the ſame footing with our noble ſyſtem of Newtonian philoſophy. It is not derived from any hypotheſis which experiments are tortured to ſerve, but the reſult of repeated effects from certain cauſes.

Long before the French had illuminated all Europe with the true rules of the drama, our Johnſon knew and practiſed them to a greater perfection than the moſt diſtinguiſhing academician ever wrote of them in ſpeculation.---Johnſon, at a time when critical learning was as ſtrange in France as in Barbary, did what no Frenchman ever was able to do. He produced regular plays of five acts, complete in the unities of place and characters, and ſo complete in the unity of time, that they are acted upon the ſtage in the ſame time which the ſame ſtory would have taken up in real life. Where then is the merit of the French critical diſcoveries when an Engliſhman has ſo much the ſtart of their academy, and ſuch advantages in the execution?

But Johnſon had an underſtanding which raiſed him next to genius. He was in the drama what Pouſin is in painting. He ſtudied the works of the antients to ſo much perfection, that his drawing, though dry, is always correct; and his attitudes, however uncouth, are always juſt. Hence, whatever he took from living manners, (of which he was ſparing) was complete in its kind; while his force of judgment, and obſervation of proportion, give a warmth, ſometimes, to his colouring, as pleaſing as when it is the reſult of nature itſelf.

Pardon this digreſſion in favour of a poet, whom I admire rather than love: But who is ſo

un-

unequal to himfelf, that when he rambles from that feverity which is fo peculiar to himfelf, you cannot find in Johnfon the fmalleft veftige of his merit ; fo entirely was he fupported upon the ftilts of clofe obfervation of nature, and ftrict application to ftudy.

EVEN the bird of nature, Shakefpear, when he neither foars to elevation, nor finks to meannefs, flies with balanced pinions ; he fkims the level of dramatic rules ; and his Merry Wives of Windfor demonftrates how much he acted againft his better judgment, when he ftretched his wings into the extravagance of popular prepoffeffions.

THIS laft expreffion brings me to a decifive obfervation. ---- Perfius, applying to moral characters, fays, " Ne te quæfiveris extra :" To the reproachful experience of our own country the reverfe is proper, when applied to intellectual characters. It is FROM WITHOUT that we are to feek for the reafon of an abfurd conduct in many of our Englifh authors, and Shakefpear in particular.

BY the expreffion FROM WITHOUT, I mean the tafte of the courts, and the people, to whom the poets wrote ; and what it was with regard to the theatre, a fhort review will exhibit.

WE are to date the revival of claffical tafte in Italy, and of claffical learning in England, from the reign of Henry VIII. That prince affected to be a fcholar, and had one quality in common with other tyrants, that he was as fevere upon the rivals of his learning, as upon the enemies of his government. The only two men of wit about his court, the earl of Surry and Sir Thomas More, loft their heads upon a fcaffold, and had Erafmus been Henry's fubject, he probably would have

shared

shared in their fate, and in that of Fisher and Cromwell. But as to learning, Henry was an ignorant pedant; it was confined to school divinity; nor do we know that he had the smallest relish for works of wit or genius. Yet during all his reign the people had their panem et circenses, " their plays and pastimes." They had their entertainments, not indeed exhibited upon the stage, but in justs and tournaments, in pageants, in largesses, and in conduits running with wine and hyppocras. When the public is liberally entertained, as they were in Henry's time, with such exhibitions, they soon forget the stage; nay, the feats of arms, and the pomp of pageants dwell so strongly on their minds, that when they are brought to theatrical entertainments, those are the first objects for which they send their eyes abroad.

EDWARD the sixth had but a narrow education; and, by what appears from his puling letters, yet extant, he had the same aversion or indifference as to works of wit as his father had. But the same public entertainments, though more rare, were, in his reign kept up to the people.

DURING the six years gloomy reign of Queen Mary, the passion of the people for pompous exhibitions was redoubled by the great influx of Spaniards, who formed the manners of the court, and encouraged the passion of the public for diversions that were so dear to themselves.

SUCH was the taste of the nation at the accession of Queen Elizabeth, who was a woman of wit as well as sense. But her sex discouraged, and her inclinations disliked, the martial entertainments so lately in vogue. She countenanced the patrons of the drama, and its poets began, though languidly, to rear their heads. Theatrical entertainments,

ments, however, in the beginning of her reign were but few. But the queen and her maids of honour made a ſhift to pleaſe themſelves with the few that were; and among the reſt with the play of Palamon and Arcite, in which was introduced a ſpecial good imitation of a pack of hounds in full cry.

WHILE the ſtage was thus over-run with ignorance, impertinence, and the loweſt quibble, our immortal Shakeſpear aroſe. But ſuppoſing him to have produced a commiſſion from that heaven whence he derived his genius, for the reformation of the ſtage, what could he do in the circumſtances he was under? He did all that man, and more than any man but himſelf, could do. He was obliged, indeed, to ſtrike in with the peoples favourite paſſion for the clangor of arms, and the MARVELLOUS of exhibition; but he improved, he embelliſhed, he ennobled it. The audience no longer gaped after unmeaning ſhew. Pomp, when introduced, was attended by poetry, and courage exalted by ſentiment. But are we to imagine that Shakeſpear could reform the taſte of the people into chaſtity? no; they had the full, the wanton, enjoyment of his genius, when irregular; and they were both too uninformed, and too incontinent, to exchange LUXURY for ELEGANCE.

THIS would, undoubtedly, have been the caſe, even ſuppoſing Shakeſpear to have attempted a reformation of the drama. But I believe he attempted none. His houſes were crouded; his applauſe was full, and his profits were great. His patrons were pleaſed with the conduct of his plays: Why then ſhould he attempt a reformation, which, with the public, muſt have been impracticable,

cable, and, to his own intereſt, might have been detrimental.

But, notwithſtanding all this, where is the Briton ſo much of a Frenchman as to prefer the higheſt ſtretch of modern improvement to the meaneſt ſpark of Shakeſpear's genius. Yet to our eternal amazement it is true, that for above half a century the poets and the patrons of poetry, in England, abandoned the ſterling merit of Shakeſpear for the tinſel ornaments of the French academy. Let us obſerve, however, to the honour of our country, that neither the practice of her poets, nor the example of their patrons, could extinguiſh in the minds of the people, their love for their darling writer. His ſcenes were ſtill admired, his paſſions were ever felt; his powerful nature knocked at the breaſt; faſhion could not ſtifle affection; the Britiſh ſpirit at length prevailed; wits with their patrons were forced to give way to genius; and the plays of Shakeſpear are now as much crowded as, perhaps, they were in the days of their author.

Nothing has contributed more to the reproachful, the ignominious, faſhion of neglecting Shakeſpear's manner, than the not underſtanding aright the character of that pride of human genius. A young gentleman naturally of a fine turn for letters, goes to the univerſity, where the amuſements of wit mingle with, nay often lead, his other ſtudies, and one of the firſt things his tutor tells him is, That all poetry is, or ought to be, an imitation of nature; and he confirms this doctrine by a number of paſſages from poets, antient and modern. This agrees perfectly well with all the flimſy French diſſertations, or Engliſh ones ſtolen from the French, which fall into his pupil's hands upon the ſubjects of delicacy, taſte, correctneſs,

rectnefs, AND ALL THAT. When his head is
quite warm with their notions, and when he ima-
gines his tafte, or fomething which he takes to be
tafte, is entirely formed, he applies his rules to
Shakefpear, and finds many of them not anfwer.
He is foon after turned over to a Swifs or a Scotf-
man, who LEADS him to travel; and in France
he has all his notions of delicacy confirmed and
rivetted. He returns to England, where he hears
the praifes of Shakefpear with filent contempt;
he tacitly pities every man who loves fo unnatural
an author, and burfts for an opportunity to dif-
charge his fpleen among his French and foreign
acquaintances.

IN reality, the gentleman is not to be blamed.
He proceeds upon a maxim, which, however
true when applied to moft other writers, fails in
Shakefpear.

SHALL I attempt to give the reafon of this?
It is not Shakefpear who fpeaks the language of
nature, but nature rather fpeaks the language of
Shakefpear. He is not fo much her imitator, as her
mafter, her director, her moulder. Nature is a
ftranger to objects which Shakefpear has rendered
natural. Nature never created a Caliban till
Shakefpear introduced the monfter, and we now
take him to be nature's compofition. Nature never meant that the faireft, the gentleft, the moft
virtuous of her fex, fhould fall in love with a
rough, bluftering, awkward Moor; fhe never
meant that this Moor, in the courfe of a barba-
rous jealoufy, and, during the commiffion of a
deteftable murder, fhould be the chief object of
compaffion throughout the play. Yet Shakefpear
has effected all this; and every figh that rifes,
every tear that drops, is prompted by nature.

NATURE

Nature never defigned that a complication of
the meaneft, the moft infamous, the moft execrable
qualities fhould form fo agreeable a compofition,
that we think Henry the fifth makes a conqueft
of himfelf when he difcards Jack Falftaff. Yet
Shakefpear has ftruck out this moral contradiction, and reconciled it to nature. There is not a
fpectator who does not wifh to drink a cup of
fack with the merry mortal, and who does not
in his humour forget, nay, fometimes, love, his
vices.

Give me leave farther to obferve, that beauties
have, in Homer and other authors, been magni-
fied into miracles, which, without being noted,
are more perfect, more frequent, and better
marked in Shakefpear, than in Homer himfelf.

To what extravagance has that father of antient
poetry been juftly raifed, for making fo many
of his heroes extremely brave, yet affigning to
each a different character of courage. But to
what perfection has our heaven-inftructed Englifhman brought this excellency which the French
critics are fo proud of having difcovered in Homer? He has not confined it to courage, but
carried it through every quality. His fools are
as different from one another as his heroes. But
above all, how has he varied guilty ambition in
a fpecies fo narrow of itfelf, that it feems impoffible to diverfify it. For we fee Hamlet's father-
in-law, Macbeth, King John, and King
Richard, all rifing to royalty by murdering their
kindred kings. Yet what a character has Shakefpear affixed to every inftance of the fame fpecies.
Obferve the remorfe of the Dane, how varied it
is from the diftraction of the Scot: mark the con-
fufion of John, how different from both; while
the

the clofe, the vigilant, the jealous guilt of Richard is peculiar to himfelf.

I SHALL now proceed in the review I undertook, that I may at laft come to the main defign of thofe pages, which was to prove the different conduct of a great genius and a fine poet, that character which has fo long ftifled dramatic excellency among us in tragedy.

JAMES the firft with much reading had but little knowledge, and with fome wit, no tafte. His minifters, or rather his favourites, were dunces and rafcals, and matters of wit were indifferent to them. They were, however, glad of every occafion to encourage every thing that could divert the public attention from affairs of ftate, and therefore they did not difcourage the ftage. They left that entirely to the patronage and management of the people. Hence it is that in all the reign of James the firft we find the theatre upon an excellent footing, and, fo far as we can judge, furnifhed with the beft fet of actors that ever adorned any one nation at any one time. In fhort, as to the drama, the public rather acquired a better tafte than it had under queen Elizabeth. The ftrength of Shakefpear, the regularity of Johnfon, the genteel manner of Fletcher, were all encouraged, and each had his juft proportion of applaufe ; nor am I fure whether this was not the period in which, take it all in all, England did not fee her ftage in its higheft perfection.

THE court of Charles the firft was too ftately, too precife, too prudifh, to allow the freedoms that prevailed in the laft reign, and, among other narrow-hearted reformations, that of the ftage took place. For, the king knowing too much and too little to encourage the true drama, wanted to have it fo very moral as to be infipid.

Hence

Hence the mafques which prevailed fo much a-
bout this time. They had been in ufe during the laft
reign, and, when well executed, they are far from
being a taftelefs entertainment. The two queen
conforts of England, being foreigners, encouraged
them as beft adapted to fpeak to the eyes. Under
James, they were confined to private parties in
the queen's apartments. But Charles, who was a
paffionate admirer of uniformity, brought almoft
all the noblemen of his court to affect them, to
the infinite prejudice of the ftage. But the di-
ftractions of this reign foon frightened the peopl
from all public diverfions, nor did they recover
till the reftoration of Charles the fecond.

THIS monarch had wit and fenfe. But, having been
abroad ever fince he attained to manly age, he had no
opportunity of cultivating what by nature he certainly was inclined to, I mean the patronage of genius.
Having loft the habit, he forgot the inclination;
but nature recurred fometimes fo ftrongly upon
him, that he was by fits munificent to literary
merit. Dryden certainly tafted of his bounty.
But in the main Charles was fcandaloufly neglect-
ful of authors, with whofe works he was charmed,
and to whofe wants he was no ftranger : witnefs
Butler and Otway. But where he was deficient,
his brother, the duke of York, though naturally
a frugal heavy prince, fupplied with his bounty.
Otway was often relieved by him; he almoft fupported Dryden; and to Wycherly he gave, at
one time, fifteen hundred pounds, befides per-
fuading his brother to fettle an handfome annuity
upon him for travelling abroad with the duke of
Monmouth.

BUT the duke of York, from this well-timed
liberality, reaped vaft political advantages. For
during the national combuftion againft his perfon
and

and right, he had the ftage, then the darling, the only entertainment, of the public, on his fide. He had the beft writers in the nation to undertake his caufe; he had the ableft fpeakers in parliament to defend his title.

But after all, I muft not diffemble that there was then a deteftable licenfing act, which did not expire till after the revolution. This act, however, had little or no force during the hotteft fits of the political difputes that then prevailed. The houfe of commons oppofed the duke of York fo violently, that the king being too wife to ufe any ftretch of power, every thing againft the duke had free vent. Nay the danger in writing was at laft thrown upon his fide of the queftion, and l'Eftrange was actually, for fome time, muzzled by the parliament.

During this long æra of wit, the drama ftill was without correctnefs. The genius of Otway himfelf did not cultivate thofe fcenes which it adorned. The patrons of wit were men of little or no tafte. They were pleafed indifferently with whatever pleafed the public. The dedications of poets were addreffed, not to merit, but to munificence; while the public itfelf was fo whimfical in its tafte, that one fashion of wit fcarcely lafted a moon. The poets on the other hand who fubfifted on the players and the bookfellers, as both thefe laft did upon the public, were obliged to conform to the prevailing tafte. Sometimes plays in blank verfe were the mode; fometimes in rhyme; one week deep tragedies, another, fmutty comedies, and a third, tragi-comedies, prevailed. The poets were ty'd down to the drudgery of fafhion; and to fit the players with every fort and fize of the commodity in vogue.

Hence

HENCE it is, that we find Dryden, in his admirable prefaces, dedications, and differtations, veering from point to point of criticifm. He had every quality of genius, he had every accomplifhment of learning , yet, with thofe advantages, how little of his dramatic excellency deferves mention. His merits however as a dramatic poet claim we fhould not forget, that in the ftory of Œdipus he has in that play reprefented his hero in all the characters which coft the antients fo many feparate characters to draw; for we fee him in Dryden, a king, a lover, a fond hufband, and a defperate madman. We are to remember that fome paffages of his Anthony and Cleopatra foften even the graces of Shakefpear; that his character of Dorax in Don Sebaftian is finely defigned; and that the tragical part of his Spanifh Friar is brought to a cataftrophe, at once, noble and natural.---Of what great, of what little, things, was not Dryden capable! If in him the public loft a genius for tragedy, it gained a poet of the firft rank in every other province of the mufes. But all his failings were owing to the vicious tafte of the nation. For after he had fhewn what he could do with encouragement, he was compelled to turn all his fine parts to the mercenary drudgery of flattering, and following through right and wrong, dull patrons, and a whimfical public.

LEE was another perifhed genius of thofe times. That he had at leaft dramatical fire is plain from what he wrote. It is likewife certain, that he could both feel and defcribe diftrefs; qualities, which of themfelves ought to give more pleafure than all the faultlefs regularity, and fine poetry of fucceeding tragedies.

WE

WE shall now proceed to the period, (a mighty
blank it is,) to the acceffion of George the fecond
from that of King William, from whence we may
date the decay of tragic genius in poetry. I am
afraid neither Row nor Addifon can wipe that reproach from this period. But what it then loft
in one branch of the drama it gained in another.
For England then faw her comic fcene brought
to perfection. To fuch perfection, that nature in
giving it feems to have exhaufted her ftock of
dramatic talents. The fame encouragement was
then given to tragedy, but the public had not the
fame tafte for the one fpecies as for the other.
The difpute between the antients and the mo-
derns, which in itfelf was idle and immaterial,
came over from France and infected our great
men, who moft of them either had wit, or were
its profeft patrons. The favourers of French
poetry then crawled out, and in that fummer of
their days, under the pretext of CORRECTNESS
helped to extinguifh SPIRIT. The cry againft the
popular tafte of poetry during the late reigns, became now more and more in fashion. Minifters
took up the pen to ridicule Dryden, ftatefmen employed their talents to recommend the academy.
England became a party in a French difpute.
France by her arts avenged herfelf of our arms;
our men of wit admitted her to be an arbiter,
without feeming once ro reflect that England
had produced a Shakefpear, a name which muft
have been decifive in the difpute, and which ought
to ftrike dumb all advocates for any other fupe-
riority in the province of the drama.

POWER is decifive in wit as in politics, when,
like the minifters of king William and queen
Anne, it is munificent and affable, and encourages
what

what it loves. Correctnefs was now all the mode. I fhall confine myfelf to the influence which this had upon tragedy alone.

IT is within the compafs of almoft every writer's abilities to be correct. He who has no other perfection may attain to that; and it muft be owned, in thofe days to have covered a multitude of faults. To exemplify this in our modern tragedies would be endlefs. Its effect was, that correctnefs was firft looked upon to fupply the place of poetry, and then poetry that of genius. Correctnefs without fpirit is a diftinction underftood by every body, but that of poetry without genius, is what I am now bound to eftablifh.

THE firft thing then a poet does, after he gets the fubject of a tragedy, is to form his characters and then his conduct. He next makes a kind of a profe anatomy of his play, and then he fits down to give it expreffion, the flefh and blood of his performance. But in what follows the genius and the poet differ, and here we fhall take them both up.

THE genius forgetting that he is a poet wraps himfelf up in the perfon he defigns; he becomes him; he fays neither more nor lefs than fuch a perfon, if alive and in the fame circumftances, would fay; he breathes his foul; he catches his fire; he flames with his refentments. The rapid whirl of imagination abforbs every fenfation; it informs his looks; it directs his motions. Like Michael Angelo, who, when carving any great defign, wrought with an enthufiafm, and made the fragments of the marble fly round him, he is no longer himfelf; he flies from reprefentation to reality;

reality; with * Shakefpear, he treads the facred ground; he furveys the awful dome; he does not defcribe, but converfe, with the ftalking ghoft, and the lawrelled dead; the hallowed vaults re-echo his fteps, and the folemn arches repeat his founds.

THE genius that is not fo ftaunch as not to ramble after the moft inviting purfuit, after the fineft fentiment, that fprings in the field of fancy, finks into poetry. A g eat genius never can be diverted from its immediate object. It does not perhaps keep up the fame intenfenefs in all the under characters of the fame play. But that is immaterial. It is fufficient if one or two cha-racters, at moft, in a play, are thus worked up; nor is it one of the leaft faults of our modern dra- that the manners of the under characters are marked too ftrongly. The practice of the an-tients, and a greater authority than the antients, that of Shakefpear, was otherwife. Among the Greeks, their Œdipus, their Iphigenia, their Philoctetes, in their feveral plays, fill up all the meafure of diftrefs, and employ all the force of attention. Shakefpear has indeed in one play very ftrongly marked one under character, I mean that of Iago in Othello; but the high finifhing of the principal one required it, and none but a ge-nius like Shakefpear could have executed fuch a plan. In Julius Cæfar, the chief character, which I take to be that of Brutus, is drawn to his hand in hiftory, as is that of Caffius; and therefore he had lefs difficulty in executing them to fuch high perfection. But this conduct, eafy as it was to

* Alluding to the known tradition that Shakefpear fhut himfelf up all night in Weftminfter Abbey when he wrote the fcene of the ghoft in Hamlet.

Shake-

Shakefpear, obliged him to throw the greateft
chara&er that ever nature formed into an under
part. The figure which Cæfar makes in that play,
is that of formal, empty pomp; and we fee the
poet has rid his hands of him as foon as he could,
that he might have the more leifure to attend his
favourite Brutus.

THIS leads me to obferve, though I have the
prepoffeffion of a whole age againft me, that
there is not the leaft neceffity for the chief per-
fonage in a play to have either courage, wifdom,
virtue, paffion, or any other quality, above what
is to be found in his real hiftory, or in common
life. It is a fign of a poverty in genius when a
poet invents a drefs of good or bad qualities for a
favourite chara&er. The antients always brought
the fame men upon the ftage, which they faw in
the world. But the French and the modern
Englifh in their tragedies have peopled the poetic
world with a race of mortals unknown to life.
This aiming at fuper-eminent qualities, were
there no other, is a proof of the defe& of genius ;
but the eternal pra&ice of the French has, in modern times, given it a fhameful fan&ion.

THE field of imagination lyes higher than that
of truth, and our modern poets generally take
advantage of the ground to mount their Pegafus.
But Shakefpear, like his own winged Mercury,
vaults from the level foil into his feat.

He has fupported the chara&er of Hamlet entirely by the force of fentiment, without giving him any of thofe ftrong markings,
which commonly form the chief modern perfon-
age in a tragedy. He has not even made ufe of
thofe advantages, with which the great hiftorian
from whom he took his fubje& might have furnifhed

nifhed him. He has omitted part of the marvellous to be met with in that writer, but has
made excellent ufe of the following beautiful defcription of Hamlet's madnefs. Falfitatis, fays
Saxo, Enim (Hamlethus) alienus haberi cupi-
dus ita aftutiam veriloquio permifcebat, ut nec
dictis veracitas deeffet nec acuminis modus vero-
rum judicio proderetur. "For Hamlet abhor-
"ring the imputation of a lye, fo mingled cun-
"ning with truth, that what he faid was neither
"void of veracity, nor could the meafure of his
"wit be betrayed by the difcoveries of his fince-
"rity." Where is the poet but Shakefpear,
who could have worked fo infipid a character into
life by the juftnefs of reflection, and the ftrength
of nature, without applying thofe colours, which
an inferior genius muft have ufed to mark a principal figure *. All that we fee in Hamlet is a
well-meaning, fenfible, young man, but full of
doubts and perplexities even after his refolution is
fixed. In this character there is nothing but what
is common with the reft of mankind ; he has no
marking, no colouring, but its beautiful drawing,
perhaps, coft Shakefpear more than any one figure
he ever attempted.

In like manner Macbeth is the fame in Shakefpear as in Boethius and Buchanan. The poet
keeps to the hiftorian's fable and characters. Ani-
mus etiam Macbethi, fays the hiftory, per fe fe-

* It may be fome fatisfaction to the reader to know that
Shakefpear has taken from the Danifh hiftory the whole of
Hamlet's difguifed madnefs ; the friendfhip betwixt him and
Horatio who was his fofter-brother, the fcene with his
mother ; the death of Polonius ; his banifhment into England ;
his return, and his killing the ufurper. The ftory of the
ghoft was either Shakefpear's invention, or, as I am inclined
to believe, he had it from the fongs of Danifh bards which was
all the hiftory that people had before Saxo and Snorro wrote.

rox, prope quotidianis conviciis uxoris (quæ omnium confiliorum ei erat confcia) ftimulabatur "For Macbeth, of himfelf impatient, was fpurred "on by the almoft daily reproaches of his wife, his "bofom counfellor in all his defigns." How nobly has Shakefpear improved this hint! how finifhed are his characters of this wicked pair! and how artfully has he conducted and defcribed the human heart through every ftage of guilt, rifing and reluctant in the man, ready and remorfelefs in the woman.

In one of the two plays wrote by the other genius of England for tragedy, I mean the Orphan, the characters, like the fable, are not raifed above the level of common life. Diftreffed innocence is all that marks Monimia. Her brother, though a favourite part in the play-houfe, has nothing about him but what any other gentleman of the army ought to poffefs. In Otway's other tragedy, Venice Preferved, the parts of Pierre and Jaffier, and the diftrefs of Belvidera are indeed ftrongly marked, but the effects their characters produce are owing to the poet's admirable application to the experience of mankind in common life, beyond which the diftrefs of his fable does not rife ; and in bringing the woes which the guilty fuffered, home to the breaft of the innocent.

Having thus endeavoured to explain what I mean by a genius in tragedy, I fhall now proceed to the defcription of a poet ; and, if you will, a fine poet, and take him where I dropt him, when he begins to colour, and to draw his characters.

He does not fo much confult what a character would fay were he in the poet's place, as what he would fay were he in the place of the character. He does not confider fo much, how things may be

pro-

properly, as how they may be finely, said. His heroes and his princesses all speak his language, that is, the language of poetry without passion. He never touches upon an effect without describing the cause; he never starts a sentiment, but instead of considering, how the character, were it real, would express it, he consults how Virgil, Lucan, Seneca, or any great antient or modern author would turn it. He then launches out into their beauties, and gives it all their embellishments.

But above all things, he is excessively fond of definitions; no great quality comes athwart his dialogue, that we have not anatomised, and its rise and progress accounted for. He is very much enamoured when his characters are virtuous, with virtue in all her shapes; he takes occasion to recommend her from the mouth either of his hero, or some of his friends. But the misfortune is, he is extremely apt to overdo. His characters of this kind are all so very virtuous, so very brave, so very loving, and so very constant, that they exclude all failing, and all propensity to guilt, which, I will venture to say, ought to attend the most complete dramatic character, and are the true springs which captivate, engage, move, and animate the passions.

Were a modern poet to express that simple, yet fine sentiment of Otway,

" O I could love thee, ev'n in madness love thee!"

how would he disdain the baldness of the expression! how would he dissect and define, first, the lady's worthiness to the object of love, then love itself! and ten to one but he would even step into Bedlam, that he might entertain us with a
more

more lively picture of madnefs and its fymptoms. Were he to exprefs the horrors of the lady Macbeth, how would he fmile fuppofing he had never read the play, if he were told it could be done beyond what ever poet executed, or imagination conceived, only by rubbing the back of her hand, and repeating a deal of wild ftuff in her fleep! With him all muft be great, all muft be philofophy, all muft be poetry.

I CANNOT prove the truth of this obfervation better than by the example of a great poet, to which character he joined as true a judgment, and as much critical knowledge as any man ever poffeffed; I mean Mr. Addifon. That author has, to the immortal credit of his name and nation, exhibited upon the ftage a Cato; but we muft take the liberty to obferve that he is not the Cato whom Rome produced, or Shakefpear would have drawn: he is fo firm in virtue, fo fortified in philofophy, that he is above the reach of fate, and confequently he can be no object of compaffion, one great end of tragedy. The poet feems to be aware of this, and endeavours to raife compaffion in circumftances, wherein he ought of all things to have avoided fuch an attempt, in drawing the character of a profeffed ftoic. With fuch, the caufe of virtue gave fupreme happinefs, whatever was its fuccefs. The friends of the family of Cato therefore could never in the eyes of a ftoic, be touched with mifery, while embarked in fuch a caufe. Thefe, I imagine, were the real fentiments of Cato, as his illuftrious cotemporaries have drawn him; and if I miftake not, Shakefpear, without any other regard, would have attached himfelf to that character only, and have made Cato from an enthufiafm of public fpirit, like the firft Brutus, do

do fomething extremely fhocking to natural affection, and to thofe private paffions which ever
mingle with the human frame, and oppofe the
force of nature to that of philofophy. This tre-
mendous virtue formed the real character of Cato;
and we find in fact the commands of the fenate,
in the bufinefs of Cyprus, engaged him to accept
of a mean, mercenary, inhuman commiffion.

THE under characters of that admirable play
are all of them highly finifhed, and each is fit for
the qualities it poffeffes to ftand as the head character in any other tragedy. But they ftand in this
play as yews did in our old gardens, each regularly oppofing the other ; and this perhaps
was one of the means which pleafed the gentlemen
of tafte at the time it was wrote. The cool, the
fteady, the referved virtue of Portius, is oppofed
to the noble, the fincere, the open manner of
Marcus. The generous, humane, difinterefted
principles of Juba, contraft the dark, defigning,
treacherous qualities of Syphax. The foftnefs,
and candour of Lucius, are defigned to raife our
hatred for the impetuous diffimulation of Sem-
pronius. All is indeed extremely well executed,
and all bears the mark of a fine poet, but not of a
great genius.

FOR a particular inftance of the difference betwixt the poet and the genius, let us go to two
fpeeches upon the very fame fubject by thofe two
authors ; I mean the two famous foliloquies of
Cato and Hamlet. The fpeech of the firft is that
of a fcholar, a philofopher, and a man of virtue :
all the fentiments of fuch a fpeech are to be acquired by inftruction, by reading, by converfation ; Cato talks the language of the porch and
academy. Hamlet, on the other hand, fpeaks
that

that of the human heart, ready to enter upon a deep, a dreadful, a decifive act. His is the real language of mankind, of its higheft to its loweft order ; from the king to the cottager ; from the philofopher to the peafant. It is a language which a man may fpeak without learning ; yet no learning can improve, nor philofophy mend it. This cannot be faid of Cato's fpeech. It is dictated from the head rather than the heart ; by courage rather than nature. It is the fpeech of pre-determined refolution, and not of human infirmity ; it is the language of uncertainty, not of perturbation ; it is the language of doubting ; but of fuch doubts, as the fpeaker is prepared to cut afunder if he cannot refolve them. The words of Cato are not like thofe of Hamlet, the emanations of the foul ; they are therefore improper for a foliloquy, where the difcourfe is fuppofed to be held with the heart, that fountain of truth. Cato feems inftructed as to all he doubts : while irrefolute, he appears determined ; and befpeaks his quarters, while he queftions whether there is lodging. How different from this is the conduct of Shakefpear on the fame occafion !

If from this light fketch it fhould appear, that the difference I have laboured to eftablifh betwixt a poet and a genius, is juftified by the practice of our greateft modern authority, how many ftrong proofs might be brought from the works of authors either lefs deferving, or lefs celebrated.

The rules of architecture, of painting, and of poetry, are in one refpect all founded upon the fame principle. There fhould be one great object, and that object under no difadvantage from the vicinity, the multiplication, or the refemblance, or ornaments of inferior members. We fee the

effect

effect which this has upon the majeſtic ſimplicity of building ; we perceive it in the happy diſpoſition of painting ; and ſhall we be inſenſible of it in the conduct of the drama? Yet the conſtant practice of the antients has not yet inſtructed us. The French with all their pretended refinements have left the ſtage in this reſpect as gothic as they found it.

Nothing encourages bad taſte either in the authors or the judges of the drama, ſo effectually, as does pride. When we want to draw a character we reſort to models of greatneſs ; to the camp, to the court, to pageants of honour, to ſcenes of grandeur. There, the language of the world drowns the whiſpers of the heart ; there, the diſtreſs which riſes, is not that of a man but of a hero ; the elevation is that of ſtate, but not of ſentiment. Were an Œdipus with us to loſe his eyes, we would make him brave his fate, and ſuperior to his misfortune, inſtead of making him with Sophocles bewail his miſery in agonies of nature.

Otway ſucceeded by converſing with the heart alone ; and Shakeſpear was the conſtant companion of nature wherever ſhe reſided : yet I am not afraid to ſay, that when either Shakeſpear or Otway turned to other objects, that is, when they commenced poets, they make but a ſorry figure. The verſes of Otway, had he been author of nothing elſe, might, perhaps, have intitled him to a ſtate worſe than that of oblivion. Neither am I afraid to queſtion, whether the greateſt of our modern poets, and, perhaps, a poet, whoſe ſuperior, antiquity never ſaw, and whoſe equal, poſterity muſt not expect ; I ſay, had even Mr. Pope attempted to write a tragedy, he muſt have made a figure in the drama, in which,

to

to fay the beft of it, we never could have dif-
cerned the author of the ethic epiftles. There are
few of our late poets (for I fpeak not of the living) who have not attempted to fhine in tragedy, but with how little fuccefs we have already
examined. Were the principal fpeeches of their
plays to be cut out, they might pafs for excellent
blank verfe poems on fuch and fuch fubjects. But
with Shakefpear as with Homer, every fpeech is
made for the character, and not the character for
the fake of the fpeech; nor can any fentiment
be pronounced but by the character that fpeaks it:
None of the leaft proofs of a great genius, and
the ftrongeft indication how intenfely and how ab-
ftractedly he ftudied.

But after all I have faid, I am far from de-
nying the great beauty of chaftity in the drama.
The unities are now, perhaps, infeparable to its
merits, and they are fo eafily practifed, that we
could not readily forgive even the greateft genius
who fhould neglect them. But is this chaftity to
attone for coldnefs? Is good fenfe to take the
place of great fentiment, or poetry to banifh paffion.

I cannot take my leave of this fubject, without
remarking in general upon the obfervations which
the French have made as to our ftage, and as to
Shakefpear particularly. An author whofe letters
are publifhed, under the name of M. Abbe le Blanc,
and which have met with a favourable reception,
leads me to detain you longer than I intended.

The abbot in his letters refembles our modern
poets in their plays; he is a very good writer, but
a very ignorant informer: He fays to his corref-
pondent, when fpeaking of Shakefpear, " Some
paf-

" paſſages of this poet tranſlated into our lan-
" guage, cannot but give the higheſt idea of his
" merit." For my own part, I doubt extremely
of this fact; or whether, when Shakeſpear is tranſlated into another language, our ideas of his merit can be raiſed much above thoſe of the beſt
French tragedies; ſo peculiarly immediate is the
connection betwixt his language and his ſenti-
ments. But how does this ingenious Frenchman
juſtify what he has aſſerted? He gives us a
ſcene; in two thirds of which, all the ſentiment,
all the character, all the ſpirit of Shakeſpear is
crippled by miſerable rhyme. Could the Frenchman pretend to be a critic of the Engliſh taſte,
and yet be ignorant that there is not in all the
works of Shakeſpear, or any other Engliſh poet,
one rhyming ſcene in tragedy, which is read, far
leſs admired, by even the moſt indifferent judges
in England.

The abbot, next with an oblique reflection, gives
us the ſcene of Beauford upon his death-bed,
which, he ſays, riſes almoſt to horror by the
truth it contains; but had the abbot been acquainted with the hiſtory of England, he would
have given Shakeſpear the praiſe of thus ennobling
a ſingle fact in hiſtory, and giving ſuch ſtrong
dramatic characters, as are thoſe of the king and
the cardinal on this occaſion, without riſing one
tittle above the level of their true hiſtories. This
is what no genius but Shakeſpear ever could do.
Notwithſtanding the high finiſhing of all his chief
hiſtorical characters, there is not a feature, there
is not a colour, there is not a manner, nor a paſſion added, which they had not in life So
well could Shakeſpear improve without altering
nature.

WHAT

WHAT I have said of his great characters, are equally applicable to his mean ones, such as those introduced in the scene which the abbot next gives us of Cade and his rabble. Ignorant and barbarously whimsical as they seem in Shakespear's scene, they are not more so than they are in the historian's page. Though Shakespear has had the art to make all such characters superlatively detestable, yet has he not added one circumstance, or exaggerated it, beyond what he found in our annals. The abbot therefore is mistaken in giving us this scene as a specimen of Shakespear's comic. It is, in effect, a specimen of the tragic as carried by the lowest, the most ignorant, the most infamous of mankind. Was Shakespear to write now, his conduct in introducing such personages would be inexcusable; but at the time he did write, it was, perhaps, proper. He wrote to a people that even but a few years before, had in fact given him the subject; nor was Shakespear dead many years before they lived over all his scenes of civil rage, and acted in the world what he described in his theatre. His representing such a people, in the strongest, the most ridiculous, the most odious colours, could not therefore but have the best effects upon his audience, and upon the public.

THE same abbot in his 73d letter, as another specimen of Shakespear's genius, gives an extract from Titus Andronicus, a play falsely attributed to Shakespear, or, if his, so justly condemned by all men of taste in England, that it can be no specimen of the English taste. But the abbot is representing the English nation as they are at present, and has been sufficiently

ently informed, he would not have given the defects of the dead Shakefpear as inftances of tafte in the living Englifh. He would have mentioned that the Englifh in general, who have eyes either to fee or read a play, are as much fhocked with, and as much condemn, the faults of, Shakefpear; nay are as much quick-fighted to them as any Academician in France can be.

But after all, I am not quite fure, whether the French or the Englifhman would agree together on the paffages to be condemned. What the Frenchman may call low ftuff and buffoonery from his ignorance of paft Englifh manners, perhaps the Englifhman may, with much better reafon, defend as fine wit, and true humour. Nay, I will go farther, by fuppofing, what I believe, that an Englifhman under King George, and one under Queen Elizabeth, could it be poffible for them to hold converfation together, would have very oppofite fentiments, with regard to what is called Shakefpear's low wit.

In the performance which the abbot gives us, called the fupplement of genius, and which is fuppofed to be writ by an Englifh wit, the criticifms are all trite and obvious, and deferve no confideration, becaufe thofe which are juft, are univerfally known and approved of by the Englifh nation. Therefore this performance, whether the work of an Englifhman or a Frenchman, gives us as little idea of the prefent tafte in the Englifh, as of real beauties in Shakefpear: But perhaps, even in criticifm as founded both on truth and the practice of the antients, we may in many things differ widely both from the abbot

and

and his author. The practice of one stage, the French for instance, ought never to be the rule for that of another. To lash the vices or expose the follies of mankind, ought in truth to be the ends of the drama, and where the vices or follies of one nation differ from those of another, the remedies must differ likewise. But a Frenchman can have no idea of the remedy, because he is ignorant of the disease.

As to the practice of the antients, one may venture to enter the lists with any academician, and be judged by any of his body who understands Greek, whether he does not in the best comedy of Aristophanes produce a greater number of more execrable puns, more indecent expressions, and lower trifling, than there is in the worst play of Shakespear.

THE Abbe in his 39th letter has the following passage : " Before the battle of Philippi, says he, " is fought, there is a parley betwixt Brutus and " Cassius on one side, and Octavius and Anthony " on the other. By the grossness of the abusive " language they give each other at this interview, " one can't take them for Romans." This observation is far from partaking of the abbe's usual candor. It is not the want of information that can bring him into so capital a blunder as to imagine that there is in all the system of modern ribaldry, any sort of words or phrases too coarse for the politest of the Romans to use, not only in private altercations but in their most awful and decent debates. This is a character stamped upon that people by their own historians ; and the thing is liberally practised by their orators. Salust, the finest gentleman in Rome abuses Cæsar in the most gross terms ; and Cicero, the fountain of
elo-

eloquence and addrefs, has, in the open fenate, at the bar, and from the roftrum, difcharged againft the greateft men in Rome, torrents of abufe, which would pollute the ftile even of our Billingfgate.

I CANNOT have a fairer opportunity, than this prefents, for obferving how ftrongly national pre-poffeffions operate upon judgment. The abbe could have no notion that heroes could ever fall a fcolding. Had they run one another through, provided it had not been upon the ftage, they had acted very decently. But the Romans, who were at leaft as brave and as fenfible a people as the French are, thought otherwife. They employed their tongues upon one another, and their fwords upon their enemies. Hence it is that in all the glorious period of their hiftory, though we meet with many fcolding bouts amongft their heroes, we don't meet with one duel. Shakefpear feems to have been perfectly fenfible of this cha-racteriftic of that great people; and though in the fine fcene betwixt Brutus and Caffius, our players have ever made a feint towards a duel or rencounter, yet nothing could be more oppofite to the poet's meaning; it is not encouraged by one fyllable of the difcourfe, and in effect it deftroys the cool fteady temper which our author, to the honour of his judgment, has made Brutus pre-ferve.

I HAVE thought proper to throw out thofe ani-madverfions upon the abbe, whom I take to be an ingenious writer. But I cannot in juftice to the public help faying, that in what regards the Englifh ftage he is abfolutely mifinformed. His judgment of our poets and actors are equally trite and abfurd, and it is

amazing

amazing that a perfon who obferves fo well fhould know fo little, If my time permitted I could undertake to prove this in many of the abbe's other remarks upon the Englifh nation. What I have done in the above lines fell in with my fub-ject, and is a juftice due to the character of the greateft genius nature ever produced.

F I N I S.

AN
ATTEMPTE

To Rescue that

Aunciente, ENGLISH POET,
And PLAY-WRIGHTE,

Maister Williaume Shakespere,

FROM THE

Maney Errours, *faulsely charged on him,*

BY

Certaine *New-fangled* WITTES;

AND

To let him Speak for Himself, as right well he wotteth,

WHEN

Freede from the many Careless Mistakeings,

OF

The *Heedless* first *Imprinters,* of his WORKES.

By a GENTLEMAN formerly of Greys-Inn.

The Ambition of one Sort *of* Scholars *is to increase the Number of* various Lections; *which they have done to such a Degree of* obscure Diligence, *that we now begin to value the first Editions of Books, as most* Correct, *because they have been* least Corrected. Pope's *Obs. on* Homer, P. 1.

Printed for the AUTHOR,
And Sold by Messieurs Manby and Cox, on *Ludgate-Hill.*
MDCCXLIX.
[Price One Shilling and Six-Pence.]

E R R A T A.

REMARK IV. Page 22. Line 10. *read* Sc. 7.   Rem. VI.
P. 24. Note (c) l. 2. *r.* N. 8.   Rem. IX. P. 28. at bottom,
r. N. 5.   Rem. XIV. P. 33. n. (l) l. 9. *r.* P. 26.   Rem. XXIII.
P. 43. N. (w) l. 6. *r.* P. 37.   Rem. XXVII. P. 48. N. (a)
l. 4.   *r. Keep in* Tunis, *&c.*   Rem. XLV. P. 71. l. 1. *r.* ετιθει.
l. 4. *r.* ἐλασσι. l. 5. *r.* Κασσιτερου.

THE

PREFACE.

*T*HAT *the Labours of those who have made* Literal-Criticism *their Study, have been of some Use in the Republic of Learning must be allowed, in restoring to the World, the* true Reading *of those many valuable* Authors, *who had suffered Mutilation, through the Ignorance, Malice, Conceit, or Avarice, of their respective Transcribers, Editors, or Typographers; and of much more Use in moral Life, by exhibiting such numerous Pictures (for the literal Critics are no contemptible Number) of exemplary Modesty in themselves: For where can we find such shining Lessons of Humility, Candour, and Complaisance, as those which are dispersed through the Works of the* periculis nostris *Men?*

Whether we consult those who have understood Aristotle, Longinus, Horace, Scaliger, Addison, Bentley, Boileau, *and other famous* Critics *ancient or modern; or those who having only heard of them, build their happy Conjectures, on the surer Rules laid down by the* facetious

facetious Dr. Swift; *we find them alike lowly, ingenuous and polite;* Men *who knew infinitely better than the Author, what he* ought *to have* wrote; *and consequently better than the whole Tribe of Readers what he* did write: *As witnesseth that learned Clerk and verbal Critic* Martinus Scriblerus, *in his Remarks on the second Book of the* Dunciad, *where he lays down this infallible Rule.* " *Two Things there are,*
" *upon which the very Basis of all* verbal Cri-
" *ticism is founded and supported: The first,*
" *that the Author could never fail to use the* very
" best Word, *on every Occasion: The second,*
" *that the* Critic *cannot chuse but know which it*
" *is. This being granted, whenever any doth*
" *not fully content us,* we take upon us to con-
" clude, *first, that the Author could never have*
" *used it, and secondly, that he must have used*
" *that very one, which we* conjecture, *in its*
" *Stead.*" *By this Means, when this Sort of* Critics *take an Author in Hand, you have their insipid Jests, low* Puns, *and forced Explanations obtruded upon you for his; and thus, instead of raising their Ideas up to their Author, they bring his down to a Level with their own: And instead of shewing how well he has exprest himself on any Subject, or in any Circumstance; give Specimens how very ill they can behave, and how wretchedly they can perform on the like Occasion.*

No Author has suffered more by this Treatment, than our deservedly admired SHAKESPEAR: *Who, though a Modern, has been explained into Obscurity, and though he wrote in a living Tongue,*
has

has been rendered unintelligible by his commentating Editors : Who in all the Passages they have tampered with, whenever they have ventured to go further than the bare Correction of the Press ; have made the most extensive, and universal Conceiver and Expresser since Homer, *the narrowest and most confined Thinker, and Speaker. If a Thought of his, though ever so universal, can be restrained to a particular View, they are sure to do it ; and if a general Expression can be wrested to a limited Sense, they never fail to chuse one, and that the least obvious.*

Thus one, where the Poet, by the Phrase " * the most precious Square of Sense" *evidently intends to describe the utmost Perfection of Sense, (alluding to the* Pythagorean *Tenet which held a Square to be the most perfect Figure) puts a † poor, low, narrow, obscene Conundrum in his Head: While another, for* " ‡ ALL TO ALL," *a* King's *general Salutation to his noble Guests, wishing all of them might enjoy all, that could be enjoy'd ; poetically dignifying that hearty* old English *Toast, of* All we wish, and all we want ; *contends for the circumscribed Compliment of* " hail" *or good* " Health to all:" *Many Instances of this Kind might be given, but here they would be tedious.*

That the old Editions are faulty in many Places, is undoubtedly true ; but they are only common Errors of the Press, except here and there a Castration in the Fol. Editions: These had

---

* LEAR. ACT I. Sc. 2. † WARB. *Edit.* VI. 6. ‡ MACBETH. ACT III. Sc. 10.

they

they rectified, they had deserv'd Thanks of all; as Mr. Rowe *justly does, who thought* Shakespear's *Text too sacred to be disturbed upon* Conjecture; *and found his Meaning too clear, and his Expression too just, to want the Help of forc'd and harsh Abbreviations, or empty Quibbles, to illustrate the one, or polish the other. What he altered, or added, he did, as those Places seemed to him, to owe their Faults meerly to the* Carelesness *of the Printer; but attempted not to reason, or refine on the Sentiment, or Language of that Poet, who, (as Mr.* Rowe *was no bad one himself) he was conscious, in his weakest Passages, excelled him.*

Had Mr. Rowe *been more assiduous in his Collations, and pointed out the Beauties of his Author a little more copiously, (as sure none of his Successors were more capable of doing it) he had saved the Public a great deal of Trouble, and no small Expence; (though in those Respects Mr.* Theobald *and Dr.* Thirlby, *deserve both Thanks, and Praise, particularly the latter, in a very great Degree, it being greatly to be lamented, the former had not more of his Assistance, or that he made Use of any Body's else) but as Mr.* Rowe *did not, and as those who came after him, have, through a Neglect of either Modesty, or Understanding, taken such large Liberties both with* Words, *and* Sense; *they have made it necessary, to try to restore* Shakespear *to himself, in order to vindicate the Nation from the odious Reproach of having admired* "* flat Nonsense," *and* "† unintelligi-
"ble

* † Phrases much in Vogue with Messrs. *Theob.* and *Warb.*
figu-

" ble Jargon," *for upwards of a Century, nay
for near a* * *Century and a half; and to shew
that notwithstanding all these profound* Critics
*have done, the old Folio Editions of our Author,
(when cleared of the typographic Mistakes, and
their Deficiencies where they occur, supplied from
the old Quartos) are by far the best, as containing
his own genuine Thoughts and Expressions.*

*The Castrations, (tho' 'tis a Satisfaction to
have recovered them) as they were little known,
were little wanted; for*

> He that is robb'd, not wanting what is stol'n,
> Let him not know't, and he's not robb'd at all:

*nor would the rest have been requisite, but for the
forced Meanings, false Explanations, harsh Abbreviations and peremptory Determinations and
Curtailings, of those profest literal* Critics, *and*
Editors, Messrs. Theobald *and* Warburton. *One
of which, in order to engross all the Fame, with
great Humility exchanged* † *Modesty, and Prudence, with a certain* poetical Editor, *for* critical *Knowledge such as it is; and with as great
Liberality bestowed some of that, on his two*
Competitors; *and then with greater Civility,*

figuratively signifying *Shakespear*'s original Text, before it was
happy enough to engage their Attention.

* *Shakespear*'s two first printed Plays (that are now to be
met with, *viz.* the 1st, and 2d Parts of King *John*) appeared
in 1591, he himself then upon the Stage, and in all Likelihood
a Proprietor (though then but 27 Years old) as he might be when
their second Edition came out in 1611.

† Preface to *Warburton*'s Edition, p. 10, 11, 12.

abused

abuſed them for not having better: And how good he was able to furniſh them with, the World may judge, by that notable Specimen of his critical Sagacity as an Explainer, in the Beginning of * MEASURE *for* MEASURE ; *where his Friendſhip ſhines equally conſpicuous, in charging his own Blunder to Mr.* Pope's *Name: Not to mention that very new Diſtemper* " † the " Oats" *this happy conjeƈturing Gentleman has diſcovered amongſt Horſes.*

In purſuing this Attempt, Shakeſpear *alone ſhall be conſidered; and where any Ambiguity ariſes, it ſhall be explained by the Poet himſelf: Always laying this down for a Rule, that as he was inſpired* by *Nature, ſo he wrote to Nature, and prided himſelf in it; as appears in*

" *Thou* Nature *art my* Goddeſs, *to* thy Law,
" My Services are bound: ————

LEAR. ACT I. *Sc.* 4.

and as his Imagination was univerſal, ſo were his Sentiments, and Expreſſions; this is the only Key to unlock his Meaning and the trueſt Light to view him in.

If he wanted a regular Education, his natural Talents were leſs cramped or fettered; un-

---

* WARB. Edit. VOL. I. *p.* 355. *n.* 1. and *vid.* Supplement with *Can.* &c. *p.* 50. *Can.* 18. and the Example following: Where you will find Mr. *Pope* having obſerved that Play was taken from *Cynthio's* Novels, *Dec.* 8. *Nov.* 5. i. e. *Decade 8th, Novel 5th,* this Gentleman has printed it *December 8th, November 5th,* at length, being leſs aſhamed to *expoſe,* than to *acknowledge,* his Ignorance of what the Abbreviation ſtood for.

† WARB. VOL. II. *p.* 442. *n.* 3.

learned

PREFACE.

learned, uninformed, but from his own keen Ob-
servation, he scorn'd to be shackled by Rules, or,
as he beautifully expresses it, to have his

———— ———— unhoused, free Condition,
Put into circumscription *and* confine.

OTHELLO, ACT I. Sc. 4.

and as his Conceptions were general, and exten-
sive, his Language was copiously nervous, and
his Diction proper; and what he thought greatly,
he uttered nobly, and boldly.

If he was deprived of the Advantages of
School Learning, his Knowledge of Nature was
vast, and comprehensive; and by a close and
strong Application, he had made himself intimate-
ly acquainted with most of the living *Tongues of his*
Time, in many of which there were some very
good Translations *from the* Antients, *which seem*
to be the Springs, from whence he drew his Clas-
sical Knowledge: *How happily he has used it,*
appears evident from its being now a moot Point,
whether he understood the Originals or not?
Which would perhaps never have been doubted,
had not his snarling Contemporary, Ben. Johnson,
taken such Pains to insinuate the Contrary, in
order to set his own Scholarship, *in Opposition to*
Shakespear's *Fertility of* Invention: *Though*
(Learning *out of the Question,)* Ben. *himself in*
his utmost Rancour, could not help paying Ac-
knowledgments to Shakespear's *happy Endow-*
ments; as he is plainly pointed at, in the apolo-
getical Discourse at the End of the Poetaster,
addressed to the Reader.

" Now

" Now for the Players, it is true, I tax'd 'hem,
" And yet, but some ; and that so sparingly,
" As all the rest might have sat still, unquestion'd,
" Had they but had the Wit, or Conscience,
" To think well of themselves. But impotent, they
" Thought each Man's Vice, belong'd to their whole
    " Tribe :   ['gainst me,
" And much good doo't 'hem. What they've done
" I am not mov'd with. If it gave 'hem meat,
" Or got 'hem cloaths, 'tis well. That was their End.
" *Only amongst them, I am sorry for*
" *Some better Natures, by the rest so drawn*
" To run in that vile line.

Yet it must not be inferr'd, Shakespear *was so
totally ignorant, of the* Roman Poets *at least,
as some have contended for : In his* Taming of
the Shrew, *he has shewn he had read* Ovid's *first
Epistle in the Original; and in his* Titus Andronicus, Horace, *and* Seneca *the* Tragedian ;
*and many Passages are to be found in his Works,
which will abundantly prove, however he acquired his first Knowledge or Taste of them, his
Relish for their Beauties, had carried him back
to the Fountain-Head : And this even* Ben. *when*
Shakespear's *Death had made his Enmity sub-
side, allowed, though sparingly, in the Copy of
Verses prefixed to the* Folio Edition *of* 1632.

    " And though thou had'st small *Latin,* and less *Greek* ;"

*which plainly admits he knew something of each :
And it is surprising Mr.* Rowe *should so pe-
remptorily assert, in his Account of* Shakespear's
Life, &c. "*That in his Works we scarce find any
*" Traces of any Thing that looks like an Imita-
                                    " tion*

" *tion of the Antients ;*" *and yet mention his*
Comedy of Errors, *the Plot of which is appa-*
rently taken from the Menæchmi *of* Plautus ;
and in which there are several Incidents borrowed
also from the Amphytrion *of the same Author:*
And in the fifth Act, a strong Imitation of Pla-
to's Dialogues, *in the* Socratic *Manner he makes*
the Abbess *use, to draw from* Adriana, *the*
Cause of her Husband's supposed Madness: As
there is also in Titus Andronicus, *a plain Allu-*
sion to, and Imitation of,

Infandum, Regina, Jubes renovare dolorem :
Trojanas ut Opes, & lamentabile regnum
Eruerint Danai; quæque ipse miserrima vidi,
Et quorum Pars magna fui. ——— ——

ÆN. II. v. 3.

in

To bid *Æneas* tell the tale twice o'er,
How *Troy* was burnt, and he made miserable ?

TIT. ANDR. Act III. Sc. ult.

besides many others in the rest of his Plays, as
any one, by consulting the ingenious Mr. Whal-
ley's *Enquiry into the Learning of* SHAKE-
SPEAR, *will be convinced; and which, if this*
Design meets with Encouragement, shall be taken
Notice of in their proper Places.

It may be asked what Pretence there can be,
to expect Encouragement to such an Undertaking,
when the Public has been already so teazed and
tired, with Commentators on this Author? The
Answer will appear in the Title-Page: For if

his

his own Expreſſions *can be proved to convey his* own Sentiments, *there is no Room to doubt, but every Body would prefer thoſe of the* Poet, *to any the happieſt Conjectures of the moſt ſanguinary literal Critic; and that they may, the following Remarks on the* Tempeſt, *'tis ſubmitted, will prove beyond Contradiction: But if the Author of theſe ſhould be miſtaken, 'tis preſumed his Love and Eſteem for* Shakeſpear, *will procure his Pardon for this Eſſay, and his future Silence, atone for his preſent Error.*

AN

ATTEMPT

TO RESCUE

SHAKESPEAR, &c.

IN

REMARKS on the TEMPEST.

HIS Play is allowed by all Judges to be one of the ſtrongeſt Teſtimonials of *Shakeſpear*'s Poetic Power, and of the Force of his Imagination, which on the Doctrine of Enchantment (in his Time firmly believed) has raiſed ſo noble a Structure: And from ſuch immoral Agents has produced ſuch fine Leſſons of Religion, and Morality as this Play abounds with.

The Plot is ſingle; the making bad Men penitent, and manifeſting that Repentance by reſtoring a depoſed Sovereign Duke to his Dominions: With the additional Leſſon, that Patience under

Afflic-

Afflictions meets in the End its Reward, that Duke's Daughter by Marriage, being entitled to a Kingdom ; the Fable being built on this fimple Story.

PROSPERO, Duke of *Milan*, being fond of Knowledge in general, and particularly of *Magic* (which he never ufes to any bad Purpofe) that he may more clofely apply to his Studies, yields up all his Power to his Brother *Anthonio :* Who, growing fond of Rule, refolves to change his deputed Authority, into an abfolute Command ; and to that End, enters into an Alliance with *Alonfo* King of *Naples*, for his Affiftance to depofe *Profpero*, and fubftitute himfelf in his Place : In Confideration of which, *Milan*, (before free) is to become tributary to *Naples*.

As *Profpero* has been an excellent Sovereign to his People, they dare not deftroy him, nor raife an open Rebellion againft him ; but *Anthonio* is to receive fome *Neapolitan* Troops privately into *Milan*; then to feize *Profpero*, and *Miranda* his young Daughter, not three Years old, and carry them on Board a Bark ; and when they have got them fome Leagues at Sea, put them into an old and leaky Boat, without any Tackling, and commit them to the Mercy of the Waves : Which was done. But *Gonzalo*, an old *Neapolitan* Lord, who has the Management of this Affair, and is a great Friend to *Profpero*, privately furnifhes the Boat with many Neceffaries of Life, and efpecially with *Profpero*'s magical Books.

Profpero, and his Daughter, are long toft on the Waves in a violent Tempeft, but are at length brought to a defart uninhabited Ifland, formerly the Refidence of an *Algerine* Witch, famous for her Skill in Sorcery (which fhe always employed to wicked Ends) named *Sycorax*; who had been banifhed

banifhed fometime before, to this Place, where
fhe died, leaving only *Caliban* a Monfter, engen-
dered of her by a Dæmon, (a Progeny finely
imagined for fuch Parents;) and *Ariel*, an aerial
Spirit, (too good for her foul Works) inclofed in
a Pine-Tree.

The firft of thefe, *Profpero* inftructs in Language, and other ufeful Knowledge, and makes
his Houfhold Servant, treating him with great
Kindnefs ; till he attempting to ravifh *Miranda*,
is confined, and ufed harfhly, for which he medi-
tates Revenge : The other is releafed from the
Tree, and made ufeful to *Profpero* in his *Magic.*

After *Profpero* has lived twelve Years on this
Ifland, there appears on its Coafts, *Alonfo* King of
Naples, returning from the Marriage of his Daughter *Claribel*, to the King of *Tunis* in *Barbary :*
Accompanied by his Son *Ferdinand*, his Brother
Sebaftian, and many other Courtiers, amongft
whom are *Anthonio*, *Profpero*'s wicked Brother,
and the good *Gonzalo : Profpero*, knowing they are
on the Coaft, by his Art, raifes a magical *Tempeft*,
in which, they appear to be all fhipwreck'd. With
this *Tempeft* the Play opens, and is named from it.

Ferdinand, who apprehends he faw his Father
fink, is led by *Ariel* to *Profpero*'s *Cell* ; where he
fees, falls in love *with*, and (fhe alfo falling in
love with him) contracts himfelf *to Miranda.*

The King, fearching for his Son, whom he
thinks (not finding him) is drown'd ; a Confpiracy
is formed againft him, by *Anthonio*, and *Sebaftian*,
who are prevented from affaffinating him and
Gonzalo, by *Profpero :* But he and his Companions
are terrified by Dæmons, and told by *Ariel*, of
their wicked Behaviour to *Profpero* ; that to that,
they owe all their Misfortunes ; which will not
ceafe

ceafe till they repent : Whereon thofe who are guilty run diftracted.

Their Recovery ; the Detection of a Plot to murther *Profpero*, framed between *Caliban*, and *Stephano*, and *Trinculo*, two Drunkards of *Alonfo*'s Retinue ; an enchanted Mafque, to celebrate the Marriage-Contract between *Ferdinand*, and *Miranda* ; the Reftoration of the King to his Senfes, and his Son ; and of *Profpero* to his Dukedom ; with the Difcovery that all was the Effect of Magic ; fill up the whole Time of Action, which is fuppofed to be about fix Hours ; *Shakefpear* having obferved the Unities more in this Play, than in any other he ever wrote.

The Manners are mix'd, and confequently the Sentiments, and Diction ; but all proper to the Perfons reprefented, and chiefly Moral ; Teaching a Dependance upon Providence, in the utmoft Danger and Diftrefs ; and the Bleffings of Deliverance, and Reward, attending that Dependance.

The Language, eafy in the Narrative ; but where the Paffions are concerned, according to this Writer's ufual Method, fublimely bold, and figurative : Though now and then, fomething harfh in the Conftruction, and by that Means, obfcure, to a curfory Reader.

The Characters admirably fuited to their Bufinefs on the Scene, particularly *Caliban*'s ; which is work'd up to a Height, anfwerable to the Greatnefs of the Imagination that form'd it : And will always fecure *Shakefpear*'s Claim to Poetic Fame, as abounding in every Part with Imagery, and Invention, which two, are the Support, and Soul of Poetry. His Language is finely adapted, nay peculiarized to his Character, as his Character is to the Fable ; his Sentiments to both, and his Manners
ners

ners to all: His Curiofity, Avidity, Brutality, Cowardice, Vindictivenefs, and Cruelty, exactly agreeing with his Ignorance, and the Origin of his Perfon.

The Plan moftly tragical, the Faculties being operated on, by Amazement, Fear, and Pity; but not regular, being mixed with comic Interludes, and the Cataftrophe happy. The Difcovery is fimple, and allowing for Enchantment, very eafily, and naturally brought about.

The MASQUE abovementioned, may perhaps give a Mark to guefs at the Time this Play was wrote; it appearing to be a Compliment intended by the Poet, on fome particular Solemnity of that Kind; and if fo, none more likely, than the contracting the young Earl of *Effex*, in 1606, with the Lady *Frances Howard*; which Marriage was not attempted to be confummated, till the *Earl* returned from his Travels four Years afterwards; a Circumftance, which feems to be hinted at, in

If thou doft break her Virgin Knot, before
All fanctimonious Ceremonies, may
With full and holy Right be miniftred, *&c.*

ACT IV. Sc. 1.

unlefs any one fhould chufe to think it defigned for the Marriage of the *Palfgrave*, with the Lady *Elizabeth*, King *James*'s Daughter, in 1612. But the firft feems to carry moft Weight with it, as being a Teftimony of the Poet's Gratitude to the then Lord *Southampton*, a warm Patron of the Author's, and as zealous a Friend to the *Effex* Family: In either Cafe, it will appear, 'twas one of the laft Plays wrote by our Author, though it has ftood the firft, in all the printed Editions fince 1623, which Preheminence given it by the Players,

is

is no bad Proof of its being the laſt, this Author furniſhed them with.

REMARK I.

ACT I. Sc. I.

Enter a (1) Shipmaſter *and a* Boatſwain.

(1) The whole Dialogue here confiſting of *Sea-Terms,* and *Phraſes,* though not quite perfect, is by much the beſt of that Kind ever introduced on the Stage ; for unleſs where *Gonzalo* mentions the Cable, (which is of no Uſe but when the Ship is at Anchor, and here it is plain they are under Sail) there is not one improperly uſed.

REMARK II.

Ma. Good, ſpeak to th' Mariners: fall to't (2) *Yarely,* or we run our ſelves aground ; beſtir, beſtir.   *Exit.*

Enter Mariners.

Boatſ. Hey, my Hearts ; cheerly, my Hearts ; *Yare, Yare,* &c.

(2) *Yarely, Yare,*] are Sea Terms ſignifying Briſkneſs and Handineſs.

REMARK III.

Boatſ. Lay her ahold, ahold ; (3) *ſet her two Courſes off to Sea again,* lay her off.

(3) *Set her two Courſes*] This is wrong pointed ; what all the Editors in general underſtood by *Courſes* here, is ſomething difficult to conceive ; the Ship's *Courſe* is the Rhomb Line ſhe deſcribes in her Paſſage, or the Point of the Compaſs ſhe ſails upon.

upon, and the Sea Phrase for that is, *she lays up*, or
steers such or such *a Point of the Compass*; but that
could not be intended here, for she could not steer
two Courses at once: The Courses meant in this
Place are two of the three lowest and largest Sails
of a Ship, which are so called, because, as largest,
they contribute most to give her Way through the
Water, and consequently enable her to feel her
Helm, and steer her Course better, than when they
are not set or spread to the Wind. And therefore
this Speech should be pointed thus,

> *Lay her ahold, ahold*; set her two Courses; off to
> Sea again; *lay her off*.

It being a Command to set those two larger Sails in
order to carry *her off to Sea again*, she being too
near in Shore. *To lay her ahold*, signifies to bring
her to lie as near the Wind as she can, in order to
get clear of any Point, or Head of Land.

REMARK IV.
SCENE III.

Prof. The direful Spectacle of the Wrack, which
touch'd
The very Virtue of Compassion in thee,
I have with such (4) *Compassion* in mine Art,
So safely order'd, that there is *no* (a) *Soul*,
No not so much Perdition as an Hair,
Betid to any Creature in the Vessel,
Which thou heard'st crie, which thou saw'st sink.

(a) —— *that there is* no Soul,] This Passage has
been a great Stumbling-block in the Way of all
the

(4) Mr. *Theobald*, *p.* 6. *n.* 4. has chang'd *Compassion* in the 3d
Line into *Provision*, on the Authority of the first *Fol. Edit.* as
he

the modern Editors, whether *Poetical*, *Critical*, or merely *Conjectural*: All or any of which could neither *divine*, *judge*, or *guess*, that a fond Father should call a much-lov'd Daughter, whom he is, at that Inftant, praifing for, and comforting under, a Diftrefs, raifed by the very Virtue, *i. e.* the Height of her Compaffion, by the tender Appellation of *Soul*. The laft learned Editor may have his Reafons for thinking the Name too good to be thrown away upon *Women*; of whom, he has in more Places than one in his Notes, betray'd his very high Efteem, and Regard: But *Shakefpear*, who clofely purfued and copied Nature, found the Expreffion as proper, as common in fuch Incidents, and therefore ufed it: And that he fo meant it in this Paffage, will appear palpable to any one, who will be at the Pains to tranfpofe the Word thus,

I have with fuch Compaffion in mine Art,
So fafely order'd, Soul, *that there is* no,
No not fo much Perdition as an Hair,
Betid, ⸺

or even to place a Comma, or a Break after *no* in the 4th Line thus,

So fafely ordered that there is no — *Soul*,
No not fo much Perdition as an Hair
Betid, ⸺

the Senfe being clearly, *I have with fuch Compaffion in mine Art*, *fo fafely ordered the direful Spectacle of the Wrack which touch'd the very Virtue of*

he fays; but as the *Edit.* of 1632, has been chiefly followed here, the Word is not alter'd, they both conveying the fame Image of Humanity in the Speaker, and equally agreeing with the Meafure of the Verfe.

Compaf-

Compaſſion in thee, that there is no Perdition, no
not ſo much, Soul, *as an Hair, betid to any Creature
which thou heard'ſt cry in the Veſſel, which thou
ſaw'ſt ſink.* *Proſpero* was going to tell his Daughter, ſimply, no Miſchief had happened ; he ſees
her diſtreſſed with Fear and Pity ; he catches the
Tenderneſs, it riſes upon him, and he abruptly
breaks off to addreſs and comfort her, calls her
his *Soul,* and leſſens the Danger, even to not a
Hair of any of the Perſons ſhe was concerned for
having ſuffered : Which beautiful affectionate Apo-
ſtrophe, as it greatly heightens the Poetry, ſo it
proves the Poet ſtrictly attended to Nature, and
obeyed her Emotions.

Many Paſſages in this Play and others, prove
this Kind of Addreſs to the Perſon frequent with
him, as in this Scene.

> *Mir. Why did they not*
> *That Hour deſtroy us ?*
> *Proſ. Well demanded,* Wench,
> *My Tale provokes that Queſtion,* Dear, *they durſt not.*

and a little after to *Caliban* ;

> ———— *When thou did'ſt not,* Savage,
> *Know thy own Meaning ;* ————

and again to him ;

> *Fetch us in Fewel, and be quick (thou wert beſt)*
> *To anſwer other Buſ'neſs. Shrug'ſt thou,* Malice ?

and in the *Merry Wives of* Windſor ;

> *Albeit I will confeſs, thy Father's Wealth*
> *Was the firſt Motive that I woo'd thee,* Anne, &c.
>   Act II. Sc. 4.

                                              And

And frequently ufes Soul in Praife and Affection :
As in this Play ;

> ———————— and the fair Soul herfelf
> Weigh'd between Loathnefs and Obedience, at
> Which end the Beam fhou'd bow : ————————

ACT II. Sc. 1.

and in the *Midfummer Night's Dream* ;

> Stay, gentle Helena, hear my Excufe,
> My Life, my Soul !

ACT III. Sc. 7.

Notwithftanding which, Mr. *Theob.* p. 7. n. 5. (and
Mr. *Pope* follow'd him) chang'd Soul into *Foyle*,
(the Proof quoted for which, out of this Play,

> ———— —— but fome Defect in her
> Did quarrel with the nobleft Grace fhe ow'd,
> And put it to the Foyle ; ———— ——

ACT III. Sc. 2.

fhews *Shakefpear* ufed the Word in its common de-
preciating Acceptation ; and not for " *Damage,*
" *Lofs,* or *Detriment,*" fuftained) when the Traces of
the Letter might have been followed nearer in *Soyl,*
and with better Authority of Context ; *Ariel* in the
Scene following this Speech, faying,

> On their fuftaining Garments, not a Blemifh,
> But frefher than before. ————————————

And *Gonzalo* in the next Act, telling the King

> Our Garments being (as they were) drench'd in the Sea,
> hold notwithftanding their frefhnefs, and gloffes ; being
> rather new dy'd than ftain'd with falt Water.

Mr. *Warburt.* indeed, *p.* 7. makes an Elifion in the
Word *ordered,* and retains Mr. *Rowe's* Word *loft* ;

So

So safely order'd that there is no Soul loft,

but without any Acknowledgment where he obtained that Reading : But this helps not either Verfe or Reading ; befides deviating greatly from *Shakefpear*'s Manner of Expreffion, to fink from a *Soul*, to a *Hair*, as he does in the next Line.

REMARK V.

Prof. ———— he being thus lorded,
Not only with what my Revenue yielded
But what my Power might elfe exact ; (b) *like One*
Who having into Truth, *by telling of it,*
Made fuch a Sinner of his Memory,
To credit his own Lie, he did believe
He was, indeed, the Duke ; ————

(b) ———————— *like One*
Who having into Truth,] This Mr. *Warb. p.* 10. *n.* 6.
has changed thus,

———————— *like one*
Who having unto truth *by telling* oft, *&c.*

but it is to be wonder'd this Gentleman (as he is very fond of Elifions, and thofe none of the fmootheft) fhould not fee it was neceffary to add a [*t*] to telling, thus, by *telling't oft*, that there might be fome Government in the Sentence ; for as it ftands now in his Edit. it does not appear what is fo often told : But the *old Reading* may well ftand, and (notwithftanding this Gentleman's peremptory Charge of Unintelligibility) be eafily underftood of

———————— *One,*
Who having, by telling of his own Lie,

Made

Made such a Sinner of his Memory
To credit it into Truth, ————

that he has forgot it ever was a Lie, and now believes it himself ; as Mr. *Warb.* does, that he is a
great and good Critic, on very little (if any) other
Foundation or Authority.

Remark VI.

Mir. Alack! what Trouble
Was I then to you ?
Prof. O a Cherubim
Thou wa'ſt that did preſerve me ; thou did'ſt ſmile
Infuſed with a Fortitude from Heaven,
When I have (c) *deck'd* the Sea with Drops full ſalt,
Under my Burthen groan'd. ————

(c) *When I have* deck'd *the Sea,*] Mr. *Warb. p.* 12.
n. 8. changes this into *When I have* mock'd *the Sea,*
and aſſigns his Reaſons, which rather confirm the
old Reading. *Proſpero* paying the Tribute of his
Grief to the ſtormy Sea which cauſed it, *Shakeſpear* finely ſays he *deck'd,* adorned it with the
Trophies of human Weakneſs, Tears; and im-
plored the Ocean from whence his Danger aroſe,
as well as lamented his dreadful Situation thereon.
And here is a great Beauty little obſerved ; that as
the Poet makes *Proſpero* ſuperior to *Sycorax's* God
Setebos, ſo he makes him inferior to Providence ;
though as an Enchanter he can raiſe a Tempeſt,
and ruffle and diſturb the Calm of Nature, yet he
cannot lay the Storm which ſhe has raiſed : And
finely inſinuates, true Innocence alone can give
real Courage: It being the Privilege of harmleſs
Infancy, to

—— ſmile

——————— *ſmile*
As with a Fortitude infus'd from Heaven,

amidſt Dangers, which would make the ſtouteſt
Manhood ſhudder.

REMARK VII.

SCENE IV.

   Proſ. My brave, brave Spirit !
Who was ſo firm, ſo conſtant, that this Coyl
Wou'd not *infect his Reaſon?*
   Ar. Not a Soul
But felt (d) *a Feaver of the* MAD, and play'd
Some Tricks of Deſperation : ———————

   (d) *A Feaver of the* Mad,] The modern Editions, *i. e. Theob. p.* 13. and *Warb. p.* 14. read here *a
Feaver of the* MIND, but neither of them claim
the Honour of the Alteration, or think it worth
their while to mark it as one, though it certainly
conveys not near ſo ſtrong an Idea of that State
and Behaviour, *Ariel* is deſcribing, as the old
Word does; beſides deſtroying the Contraſt *in
Terminis* betwixt *Reaſon,* and *Madneſs,* which the
Poet plainly intended : And as they have produced
no Authority for their new Word *Mind,* we may
with old 1632, let *Mad* be the right Reading. A
Feaver of the Mind being propereſt underſtood,
of what is now generally called a Feaver of the
Spirits ; which renders the Perſons labouring under it low, faint, heartleſs, and dejected ; quite
unable to exert themſelves : But here the Author
ſpeaks of the greateſt Hurry of Spirits, an Idea of
preſent, imminent Danger can occaſion ; which
                              prevents

prevents them from attempting any Remedy, and makes them madly leap into the Sea, not through Hopes of Safety there, but merely to avoid the fiery Death which feemed to threaten them on Board ; which Hurry he poetically calls a Feaver, *i. e.* the very Height of *Madnefs :* And in all Probability, had his Eye on that Species of Feavers call'd a Calenture, which is always attended with a particular Kind of Delirium; making the Difeas'd look on the Sea as a green Field, and leap into it as fuch.

Remark VIII.

Ar. ——— (e) And for the reft oth' Fleet
(Which I difpers'd) they all have met again,
And are upon the *Mediterranean* (f) Flote,
Bound fadly home for *Naples* ;
Suppofing they faw the King's Ship wrack'd,
And his great Perfon perifh :

(e) ——— *and for the reft oth' Fleet,*] One of the heavy Charges againft *Shakefpear* is, his not attending over exactly to minute Circumftances in his Plots, (though he ftrictly obferved them in his Characters,) and by that Means offending Probability ; but here, he has been careful even to Nicety, to avoid that Imputation ; for had he not thus accounted for the Difperfion of the Fleet, either *Alonzo* and his People muft have had Help, or more have been fhipwreck'd with him ; either of which would by crouding the Scene, have fpoiled the Plot, and are both thus happily, and fkilfully avoided.

(f) Mediterranean *Flote*] *Flote* a *Saxon* Word for a Stream, River, or Flood ; and here ufed by the Poet for the Sea.

Re-

REMARK IX.

Prof. Ariel, thy Charge
Exactly is perform'd ; but there's more Work :
What (g) *is the Time oth' Day?*
Ar. Paft the Mid-feafon.
Prof. At leaft two Glaffes : the Time 'twixt fix and now,
Muft by us both be fpent moft precioufly.

(g) *What is the Time oth' Day?*] It is a very eafy
Thing to fay this or that is done *impertinently* ;
but Care fhould be taken that the Charge fhould
not rebound to the Accufer : Mr. *Warb.* p. 16. *n.* 2.
fays " both the Queftion and Anfwer are made
" *impertinently*" in this Paffage, becaufe *Profpero*
who afks it, in fome Degree anfwers it himfelf ;
and therefore gives the whole Anfwer to *Ariel :*
Which though it might cure the Impertinence of
the Anfwer, if it really wanted it ; is no Remedy
for that of the Queftion, which this Gentleman
leaves as he found it. But both Queftion and Anfwer may ftand as in the Fol. Edit. made by *Prof-*
pero himfelf ; who in the Hurry of his Mind,
might have forgot the general, and yet, as foon
as that was recalled to his Memory, very naturally
recollect the particular Time, even to Minute-
nefs, nothing being more common : And *Shake-*
fpear always kept Nature in his View, and purfued
her in her Irregularities as well as her Beauties.
And if this Gentleman had remembred fome of
his own Notes, he would not fure have charged
Shakefpear, or the *Player Editors*, with Impertinence, for making any one afk Queftions merely
for the Sake of anfwering them himfelf : *Vid.*
                                        WARB.

WARB. Vol. I. *p.* 110. *n.* 6.* But perhaps he makes his Forgetfulnefs an Evidence of his Wit.

REMARK X.

SCENE IV.

Enter Caliban.

Mr. *Warb.* would have done well, to explain what he meant, *p.* 19. *n.* 3. by *Antique* with Refpect to the Language of *Caliban* ; and alfo to have af-fign'd a Reafon why he calls his Character *Gro-tefque?* Becaufe there is nothing obfolete in Phrafe or Idiom in his Speech, though his Stile is pecu-liarly adapted to his Origin ; nor is there any Thing abfurd, capricious, or unnatural in his Cha-racter, taking the Doctrine of Witches, and their engendering with Dæmons (which was fully credit-ed in *Shakefpear*'s Time) for granted: And the traditionary Sentiment of Lord *Faulkland,* Lord Chief Juftice *Vaughan,* and Mr. *Selden,* that *Shake-fpear* had given a *new* Language to this new in-vented Character, will hold good, notwithftanding that Gentleman's long Note : Nor is the Affertion fo extravagant, or obfcure, as to need his Com-ment.

REMARK XI.

Prof. Abhorred Slave ;
Which any Print of Goodnefs wilt not take,
Being capable of all Ill.   I pitied thee,
Took Pains to make thee fpeak ; *taught thee each Hour*

* And many other Paffages, as *p.* 21. *n.* 5, *&c.*

One

One Thing or other ; (h) *when thou did'ft not*, Savage,
Know thy own Meaning, but woud'ft gabble like
A Thing moſt brutiſh : *I endow'd thy Purpoſes*
With Words that made them known.

(h) —*when thou* did'ft not, *Savage*] Mr.*Warb.p.* 2 1.
n. 5. changes *did'ft* into *coud'ft*, and *know*, into *ſhew* ;
following, 'tis to be preſumed (5) " *the ſevere* CA-
NONS *of* LITERAL CRITICISM;" and indeed his
Criticiſms are ſo *literal*, that he has often diſguiſed,
and more often perverted the Senſe of his Author:
And no where much more, than in this Paſſage.
Shakeſpear, he ſays, makes *Proſpero* upbraid *Caliban*, with only having taught him to *ſpeak* ; but
ſurely there is another, and a nobler Benefit here
mentioned, inſtructing him to *think :*

——— *taught thee* each Hour
One Thing or other ;

and if *Proſpero* was ſo exact and learned a Speaker,
as Mr. *Warb.* contends for, he hardly ſubſtituted
Thing for *Word*, which laſt ſhould have been the
Term uſed, if Language only had been taught : But
it is pretty plain, *Proſpero* here ſpeaks of Inſtruction
in general, which *Caliban* was totally deſtitute of
when firſt found ; without any Arrangement of
Ideas, which the Poet calls *Purpoſes* ; and ignorant of every Thing (but what the Calls of Nature
ſuggeſted to him) even of what was healthful or
hurtful for him, as well as of Language : Which
when learnt, enabled him to ſort and ſeparate his
Ideas, and know his own Purpoſes, or thoſe Meanings he had received from *Proſpero*, (as well as to
make them known to others) which before he did

(5) Pref. to *Warb.* Edit. *p.* 14.
not ;

not; and confequently the old Reading is righteft:
For as to teaching him barely to fpeak, the Benefit was apparently greater to *Profpero*, who made
him his Servant, and by that taught him to under-
ftand his Commands, without which he had been
ufelefs to him, than it could poffibly be to *Caliban*;
whofe great Caufe of Complaint is, his being
made a Slave: And tells *Profpero* but 19 Lines
before, he was thankful not only in Words, but
in Deeds, for the general Inftruction he had given
him; and upbraids himfelf for the Gratitude and
Love he had expreffed, while he was gently
treated.

———— ———— When thou cam'ft firft,
Thou ftrok'ft me, and mad'ft much of me; and woud'ft
    give me
Water with Berries in't; and teach me how
To (6) name the bigger Light, and how the lefs
That burn by Day and Night: *And then I lov'd thee,*
And fhew'd thee all the Qualities o'th' Ifle,
The Frefh-Springs, Brine-Pits; barren Place, and fertile;
Curs'd be I that I did fo.

REMARK XII.

SCENE V.

Ferd. Where fhou'd this Mufic be, in Air, or Earth?—
It founds no more; and fure it waits upon
Some God o'th' Ifland. Sitting on a Bank,
                      Weeping

(6) It has been obferved, Mr. *Pope* in thofe two beautiful Lines
in his Paftorals,
                              " *And*

Weeping (i) *again*, the King my Father's Wreck,
This Mufic crept by me, upon the Waters;
Allaying both their Fury, and my Paffion,
With it's fweet Air; ─────────

(i) *Weeping* again *the King my Father's Wreck,*]
Mr. *Warb. p.* 22, changes *again*, to *againft*, without fhewing either Authority or Reafon for it; as
indeed he could not well fhew the laft, the Phrafe
being never ufed but in Oppofition, or Expectation : And *Ferdinand*, believ'd his Father already
drowned. *Shakefpear* certainly wrote (if that critical Phrafe may be allowed) as the old Edit. have
it, *again*; poetically defcribing, the Reiteration of
that filial Grief, which, after fome fhort Ceffation,
again wept the fad Remembrance of a lov'd Father's untimely Death.

" *And what is that, which binds the radiant Sky,*
" *Where twelve bright Signs in beauteous Order lie?*

Spring, l. 39, 40.

had

In medio duo Signa, Conon : & quis fuit alter,
Defcripfit radio totum qui gentibus Orbem;
Tempora quæ meffor, quæ curvus Arator haberet?

of *Virgil's* 3d *Bucolic* in his Eye : And *Caliban's* forgeting the
Names of the Sun and Moon in this Paffage feems to have had
the fame Original, though the Phrafe is copy'd from an Author of fuperior Reputation.

R E M A R K

REMARK XIII.

ARIEL's *Song*.

Full (k) *Fathom five thy Father lies,*
  Of his Bones are Coral made :
Those are Pearls that were his Eyes ;
  Nothing of him that doth fade,
  But doth suffer a Sea-change,
  Into something rich and strange.

(k) Mr. WARB. *p.* 23. *n.* 6. is even prolix, in
justifying *Shakespear* in this Song, from *Gildon*'s
Charge of trifling ; and so far he deserves the
Thanks of the Public : Nothing being more Poetical, than this Method of fixing strongly in *Ferdinand*'s Mind, at this Juncture, the Idea of his
Father's Death ; the Belief of which, is now ab-
solutely necessary towards carrying on the Plot,
as Mr. *Warb.* very justly observes : But then, he
grossly affronts every one who can read *Shakespear*,
by asserting that he believes the general Opinion
joins with Mr. *Gildon* ; when *Ferdinand* immediately, after the Song, tells the Design of it. " *This*
" *Ditty does* remember my drown'd Father ;" and
then directly acknowledges the magical Influence,
here so beautifully supposed by the Author, to begin its Operation on the two Lovers,

  This is no mortal Business ; *nor no Sound,*
  That the Earth owns. —— ——

REMARK

REMARK XIV.

Ferd. Moſt ſure the Goddeſs,
On whom theſe Airs attend ! Vouchſafe my Pray'r
May know, if you remain upon this Iſland ;
And that you will ſome good Inſtruction give,
How I may bear me here : My prime Requeſt
(Which I do laſt pronounce) is, O you wonder,
If (1) you be *Mayd* or no ?

    Mi. No Wonder, Sir,
But certainly, *a Mayd.*

  (1) *If you be* Mayd *or no ?*] Great Critics are
frequently apt to over-ſhoot the Mark, and ſpy
Beauties, and *Blemiſhes,* where no other Eye can ;
but the Miſchief on't is, that common Underſtand-
ings, not being able to ſee Things in the ſame
Light, are apt to give them different Names, and
to call their *Flowers* Faults : As 'tis likely may be
the Caſe in this Place.
  Mr. *Warb. p.* 26. *n.* 9. (following Mr. *Pope's* Alteration, but ſure no Amendment) juſt after having taken Pains, to clear his Author from trifling,
here ſtrenuouſly endeavours to make him guilty of
the worſt Sort, *punning :* By changing the Subſtan-
tive *Mayd* [for *Maid*] into the Participle *made* ;
and has ſubjoin'd a long Note to this merry Blunder, to illuſtrate his Author's (as he calls it) pleaſant
Miſtake : For no Reaſon that appears, unleſs it is
becauſe (as *Shakeſpear* finely obſerves, on another
Occaſion)

  Conceit *in* weakeſt Minds *ſtill* ſtrongeſt works.
                  HAMLET.

                        Fo**r**

For can any one reasonably imagine *Shakespear* in this Conjuncture, on which the good or ill Fortune of *Prospero*, the chief Character of the Play, depended, cou'd so far forget himself, as to let the whole Plot stand still for the Sake of so low a Pun ? The Knowledge whether *Miranda* was mortal or not, might be proper enough to satisfy *Ferdinand*'s Curiosity, and if the latter, to obtain Protection for him ; but conduces nothing to the Business in Hand, the Marriage of *Ferdinand* and *Miranda*, and by that Match, the Restoration of *Prospero* to his Dominions ; but sure, the Knowledge whether she was single, which the Poet beautifully and justly phrases "Maid or no", was very material to that Purpose, and very natural, and extremely proper for *Ferdinand* to enquire into : He felt a growing Passion, and was willing to be satisfied as soon as possible, whether he might indulge it or not, or whether that grand Obstacle of her being already engag'd, stood in his Way? This appears clearly to be the Poet's Design, who makes both the Question and Answer, naturally proceed from the Subject, the growing Love of the two Persons, whose Affections are hurried on towards each other, by the Impulse of preternatural Powers, and not from the idle Curiosity of the one, or the ignorant Simplicity of the other.

Ferdinand sees her in Company with *Prospero*, whom he does not yet know to be her Father ; and though these are all the Persons he has yet seen in the Island, he can't tell how well it may be peopled : And is naturally apprehensive so great a Beauty must have produced the same Effect on others, he feels it has done on him ; and desires to be informed of the Consequences.

The Author confirms this Sense strongly four Speeches after, by making *Ferdinand* say to her,

O

O if a Virgin
And your Affections *not gone forth,* ————

which would have follow'd her Anſwer immediately, if the natural Surprize he was under, at hear-
ing her ſpeak his Language, and what follows
from *Proſpero*, had not prevented it, which it is
much ſo ſharp-ſighted a Critic ſhould overlook:
However, the *moral* Turn of his Note is very com-
mendable.

REMARK XV.

Ferd. ————— My ſelf am *Naples*;
Who, with mine Eyes, (ne'er ſince at ebb) beheld
The King my Father wreck'd.
    Mir. Alack for Mercy!
    Ferd. Yes faith, *and all his Lords:* The (m) *Duke of*
    Milan,
And *his brave Son*, being twain.
    Proſ. The Duke of *Milan*,
And his more brave Daughter, could (n) *control* thee
If now 'twere fit to do't —————

(m) ————— *The Duke of* Milan] Mr. *Theobald*,
p. 21. n. 11. of his Edition, objects to theſe Words,
" *The* Duke *of* Milan, and his brave Son," the
Duke of *Milan* not being ſaid to have any Son;
and therefore he thinks 'tis *Error Perſonæ:* But if
'tis conſidered as an Enumeration of ſome of the
higheſt of the Lords, who with the King ſuf-
fer'd Shipwreck, which does not neceſſarily imply being drown'd, being himſelf an Inſtance of
the contrary, it may very grammatically be referr'd
to the King's brave Son, meaning himſelf: Who
                        might

might with great propriety be reckon'd one of his Father's Lords, tho' with as great good Manners, he mentions the Duke first.

And then the Sense will be, *I am King of* Naples *myself*, who with mine Eyes (ne'er since dry) beheld the King my Father, and all his Lords wreck'd ; his brave Son, and the Duke of *Milan*, being two of those Lords. *Shakespear* made use of this harsh Construction for the Sake of the Antithesis in *Son* and *Daughter*.

(n) ———— *cou'd* control *thee*] *control* for contradict.

REMARK XVI.

Mir. O dear Father,
Make not too rash a Tryal of him, (o) for
He's gentle and not fearful.

(o) ————— *for*
He's *gentle*, and not *fearful.*] Mr. *Warb.p.* 27. *n.* 2. says, " This seems to be an odd Way of express-" ing her Sense of her Lover's good Qualities." *i. e.* Mr. *Warb.* is in some doubt whether good Breeding, and Valour, are necessary Requisites in a Gentleman, and seems to think it odd she shou'd esteem them so: And adds, " It is certain the " Beauty of it is not seen at first View ;" but sure, 'tis extremely obvious, that she plainly acknowledges in these Words, she is forcibly struck with the Humility of his Address to her ; his filial Piety, in lamenting the Loss of his Father ; and his general Civility in Conversation, till *Prospero* threatens to treat him indignantly ; and with his Courage, in doing what she had never seen before, making a Shew of Resistance against *Prospero's* Power ; and from these Qualifications, superior to

any

any she had known but in her Father, she is fearful of a Struggle between them left the former shou'd be hurt in the Action on the one Hand, or her Lover he destroy'd by Magick on the other: Thus the Poet has clearly expres'd in five Words, all the tender Fear that Duty, and a growing Affection cou'd shew, *He's gentle,* and therefore ought not to be ill treated; *and not fearful,* and therefore it may be dangerous to attempt it.

REMARK XVII.

Prof. Come on, obey:
*Thy Nerves are in their Infancy again
And have no Vigour in them.*
Ferd. So they are:
My Spirits *as in a Dream* are all bound up. (p)

(p) *My Spirits as* in a Dream, *are all bound up.*]
Mr. *Warb. p.* 29. *n.* 3. says, " this is an Allusion " to the common Sensation in Dreams, *&c.*" But he might have seen, that *Shakespear* might as well have that beautiful Passage in *Virgil,*

Ac velut in somnis *oculos ubi languida pressit
No&te quies, nequicquam avidos extendere cursus
Velle videmur.* At in mediis conatibus ægri
Succidimus; *non lingua valet,* non corpore notæ
Sufficiunt vires, *nec vox, nec verba sequuntur.*
ÆN. XII. v. 908.

in his Eye here, as the Passage in *Ovid,* he supposes him to have taken Notice of in another Scene of this Play.

RE-

REMARK XVIII.

ACT II. SCENE I.

Gonz. Befeech you, Sir, be merry : You have Caufe,
(So have we all) of Joy ! For our Efcape
Is much beyond our Lofs; our (q) *Hint* of Woe
Is common ; every Day fome Sailor's Wife,
The Mafters of fome Merchant, and the Merchant,
Have juft our Theme of Woe : But for the Miracle,
(I mean our Prefervation) few in Millions
Can fpeak like us : Then, good Sir, weigh
Our Sorrow, with our Comfort.

(q) —— *our* Hint *of Woe*,] Mr. *Warb. p.* 30.
n. 4. changes *Hint* for *Stint*; but if he cou'd have
taken the Hint, he wou'd have found the old
Reading trueft, and much the moft poetical to
exprefs the Lightnefs of their Caufe of Grief,
which, compar'd to many others, was but a *Hint,*
flight, and fmall : The Proportion of it, (to which
Stint alone can refer) it cou'd not be, for they
were but juft beginning to feel their Mifery ; and
therefore can only be intended of the Slightnefs of
it, as the true Senfe of the Word imports : Which
does not fignify or imply, " Prognoftication" or
Foreknowledge, but a faint Communication, of
fomething till then unknown, or not remembered.

R E-

Remark XIX.

Alon. (r) Pry'thee Peace.

(r) Mr. *Pope* (and Mr. *Warb.* *p.* 30. *n.* 5. applauds his Judgment, by adopting it) says, " All " this that follows from the Words ' *prithee Peace* ' " to the Words ' *you cram thefe Words into mine* " *Ears*,' &c. feems to have been interpolated (per- " haps by the Players)" but fure he did not con- fider that in this fancied Interpolation, the Poet has fkilfully open'd fo much of the Story, as was neceffary to the Plot, which preceded the Open- ing of the Play. *Sebaftian*, and *Anthonio*, found their Confpiracy againft *Alonzo*, as well on the Circumftance of *Claribel*'s Marriage in *Africa*, as on *Ferdinand*'s fuppofed recent Death ; her Diftance from *Naples*, being one main Inducement for them to undertake the treacherous Defign. Mr. *Theob.* therefore, *p.* 23. *n.* 12. has juftly exploded this Piece of Criticifm.

Remark XX.

Seb. He receives Comfort like cold Porrage.
Ant. The (s) *Vifitor* will not give him o'er fo.

(s) The Vifitor *will not give him o'er fo.*] Mr. *Warb. ibid. n.* 6. changes *Vifitor* into '*Vifer* abbre- viated for *Advifer* ; but certainly the old Reading may ftand, even in this Senfe, if this Gentleman recollects enough of the Univerfity to remember the Duty of a *Vifitor*, which is to advife and cor- rect; as *Gonzalo* is here trying to do the King's in- temperate

temperate Grief: Which *Sebaſtian*, and *Anthonio*
endeavour to ridicule, by making him aſſume the
Character of a Viſitor, or Reformer.

The Lowneſs of the Dialogue, ſo frequent in our
Poet, and in all his Contemporaries, (the learned
Ben not excepted) and which has been ſo often
lamented, and condemn'd in *Shakeſpear*, does not
in the leaſt contradict, but that it might be de-
ſign'd as a Satire by the one, as it is allow'dly by
the other, on the vicious Prevalence of that ſnip-
ſnap Wit, then ſo much in Vogue: And intended
purely to expoſe it, rather than any Fondneſs *Shakeſpear* had for it; or that tame Compliance with the
Mode, it has generally been attributed to.

And if what he makes *Gonzalo* ſay in the Cloſe
of this Scene be duly attended to, it gives a ſtrong
Turn that Way.

> *Alon. Pry'thee no more,* thou doſt talk nothing to me.
>
> *Gonz. I do well believe your Highneſs: And did it to
> miniſter Occaſion to theſe Gentlemen, who are* of ſuch ſen-
> ſible, and nimble Lungs, that they always uſe to laugh
> at NOTHING.
>
> *Ant. 'Twas you we laugh'd at.*
>
> *Gonz. Who in* this Kind of MERRY FOOLING am
> *Nothing* to you: *So you may* continue, and laugh at
> NOTHING *ſtill.*
>
> *Ant. What a Blow was there given !*

Who does not ſee, this evidently ſatirizes that
Fault, for which the Poet has been ſo often un-
juſtly upbraided?

REMARK XXI.

Gonz. I'th' Commonwealth, I wou'd by Contraries
Execute all Things: For no Kind of Traffick
Wou'd I permit; no Name of Magiſtrate;
Letters ſhou'd not be known; Riches, Poverty,
And Uſe of Service, none; Contract, Succeſſion,
Bourn, Bound of Land, Tilth, Vineyard, none;
No Uſe of Metal, Corn, or Wine, or Oil;
No Occupation, all Men idle, all,
And Women too; but innocent and pure:
No Sovereignty.
   Seb. Yet he wou'd be King on't.
   Ant. The (t) *latter End* of his *Commonwealth* forgets
the Beginning.

(t) *The* latter End *of his* Commonwealth, *&c.*]
Mr. *Warb. p.* 34. *n.* 8. ſays, " All this Dialogue is a
" fine Satire on the *Utopian* Treatiſes of Govern-
" ment;" but it may perhaps with greater Juſtice
to the Poet, be look'd upon as a Compliment to
Sir *Philip Sidney*'s *Arcadia*, and Lord *Bacon*'s *New
Atlantis:* The Praiſes being put in the Mouth of
Gonzalo, who is drawn as a good, and a wiſe Man,
and the Sneers in thoſe of *Sebaſtian*, and *Anthonio*,
two no very favourable Characters.

REMARK XXII.

   Seb. What a ſtrange Drowſineſs poſſeſſes them?
   Ant. It is the Quality o'th' Climate.
   Seb. Why
Doth it not then our Eye-lids ſink? I find
Not my ſelf diſpos'd to ſleep.

                                Ant.

Ant. Nor I, my Spirits are nimble :
They (u) fell together all, as by Confent
They dropt, as by a Thunder-ftroke : ———

(u) *They fell together all*] Mr. *Theob. p.* 29. and
Mr. *Warb. p.* 36. point this Paffage thus,

They fell together all as by Confent,
They dropt as by a Thunder-ftroke.

But if it was pointed as follows,

They fell together, all as by Confent ;
They dropt, as by a Thunder-ftroke : ———

perhaps it wou'd give a more poetic Turn to the
Defcription, by the Climax from their own Act, to
fome preternatural Caufe ; which feems manifeftly
to have been intended, by introducing *Ariel* with
folemn Mufic, which was to have only that fom-
niferous Effect, there being nothing confequent
following on his Entrance, but the fudden Drow-
finefs which fiezes *Gonzalo*, *Alonzo*, *Adrian*, and
Francifco, immediately thereon.

REMARK XXIII.

Seb. ——— And thou doft fpeak
Out of thy Sleep : What is it thou did'ft fay ?
This is a ftrange Repofe, to be a-fleep
With Eyes wide open : Standing, fpeaking, moving ;
And yet fo faft a-fleep.
  Ant. Noble *Sebaftian*,
Thou let'ft thy Fortune fleep ; die rather : Wink'ft
Whilft thou art waking.
  Seb. Thou doft fnore diftinctly ;
There's Meaning in thy Snores.

Ant.

Ant. I am more ferious than my Cuſtom; you
Muſt be ſo too, if heed me : Which to do,
(w) *Trebles thee o'er.*

(w) Trebles *thee o'er*] *Anthonio* is going to per-
ſuade *Sebaſtian* to deſtroy the King his Brother, and
ſeize his Throne; and to induce him to liſten, tells
him, what he is about to propoſe will make *Sebaſtian* three Times greater than he is, at that Juncture : And Mr. *Warb.*'s Remark, *p.* 37. *n.* 1. on the
Baronet's Alteration to " troubles thee not" was neceſſary; but it would have been but fair, to have
acknowledged who led him into that Error; for
there was a Reading nearly of that Kind long before the *Oxford* Edition came out, as may be ſeen
in Mr. *Theob.* Vol. 1. *p.* 30. *n.* 14. *in fine.*

REMARK XXIV.

Ant. ———— ———— No Hope that Way,
Is another Way, ſo high an Hope, that even
Ambition (x) *cannot pierce a Wink beyond,*
But *doubt* Diſcovery there.

(x) ———— *cannot pierce a Wink beyond*] Mr.
Warb. p. 38. *n.* 2. very juſtly corrects the *Oxford*
Edit. in this Paſſage alſo; where *doubt* is chang'd
for *Drop* : But whether *to pierce a Wink beyond* ſig-
nifies barely to ſee or diſcern, will admit a Query?
Ambition prompts Men to look forward from the
Point they poſſeſs, to ſomething that appears more
advantagious; and to uſe their utmoſt Endeavours
either by Force or Fraud to obtain it : And *Anthonio* here, tells *Sebaſtian*, (whoſe ambitious Nature
he is acquainted with, and endeavouring to work
on) that it is impoſſible for him with his utmoſt
Pene-

Penetration to see any Prospect of Greatness beyond what the present Hope affords him, but what
must be very dubious ; *i. e.* If he lets slip the Opportunity which now offers, by killing the King,
(his Son being drown'd, as they supposed) to se-
cure the Throne of *Naples* to himself ; it was very
doubtful whether any other would ever offer to his
Hope : And not as Mr. *Warb.* expresses it, doubt
whether that Hope was a Hope or not ; which is
not very wide of the Absurdity he charges on the
Baronet's Alteration.

REMARK XXV.

    Ant. Then tell me
Who's the next Heir of *Naples?*
    Seb. Claribel.
    Ant. She that is Queen of *Tunis*; she that dwells
Ten Leagues beyond Man's Life ; she that from *Naples*
Can (y) *have no Note*, unless the Sun were Post,
(The Man i'th' Moon's too slow) till new-born Chins
Be rough and razorable ; ———

    (y) *Can have no Note*] We are told by Mr. *Warb.*
p. 38. *n.* 3. that Mr. *Pope* says this means " no Ad-
" vice by Letter"; and he not contradicting it, ap-
proves it : Thus all the Commentators cramp the
extensive Scope of the Poet's Expression, to the
narrow Limits of their own confin'd Ideas.
    Shakespear here takes in the whole View of
their then respective Situations : *Ferdinand*, drown'd
(as is imagined) *Claribel* married in *Tunis*, out of
the Reach of Information unless sent expresly ;
there being great Improbability, not to say Im-
possibility, she should hear by Report her Father
                      and

and Brother were dead: *Alonzo*, going to be deftroy'd in an uninhabited Ifland; and *Sebaſtian*
getting from that Ifland, (if ever he gets off)
King of *Naples*; and both till, and after his Ar-
rival there, preventing by his Authority, any Em-
baffy, (which, 'tis fubmitted, is rather a properer
Way of notifying the Acceffion to a Throne, than
a Letter by the Poft) from being fent to *Tunis*;
and confequently *Claribel*, from knowing her Right,
till *Sebaſtian* had fecurely fix'd his Power, unlefs
fhe fhould learn it by Rumour, which the Poet fup-
pofes fhe could not do Time enough to be of any
Ufe: And this is his Meaning of *no Note*; for
Shakeſpear was enough acquainted with *Geography*,
to know that a Courier might go from the remoteft
Part of *Italy*, to the utmoft known Extent of
Barbary, long before ————————

———— new-born Chins
Grew rough and razorable, ——

if the *Diſtance* was the only Impediment.

And here the Poet has fhewn his great Skill in
Human Nature: *Anthonio*, whofe Tendency to Evil
is defcribed by himfelf in this Scene, forgets, in
his ftrong Propenfity to Power and Mifchief, all
the Circumftances that make againft him: The being in a defart Place; nothing for his Monarch
(when he has made him) to rule over, or to be en-
rich'd by; nor any reafonable Profpeĉt of ever
getting out of that Situation: And beyond even
this, he forgets that the reft of *Alonzo*'s Fleet,
(which he may believe have efcaped the Storm, as
he fees none of them wreck'd) are on their Paffage homeward, with the melancholy Tidings of
the Lofs of their King and Prince; the Confe-
quence

quence of which muſt naturally be, the Vacancy in
the State would be filled up, and all ſettled, before *Sebaſtian*, in all human Probability, could put
in his Claim.

REMARK XXVI.

Ant. ———— ———— (z) She *that* from whom
We *all* were Sea-ſwallow'd; tho' *ſome* caſt again;
And *by that Deſtiny* to perform an Act,
Whereof what's paſt *in* Prologue; what to come,
In yours and my Diſcharge. ———— ————

(z) *She* that *from whom*, &c.] The whole Tribe
of *modern Editors*, alter this Paſſage thus ;

———— ———— *She* from whom
We were Sea-ſwallow'd; tho' ſome caſt again,
May *by that Deſtiny perform an Act,*
Whereof, what's paſt is Prologue; what to come,
Is *yours and my Diſcharge.* ———— ————

But have not thought fit to ſhew, either *Authority*
or *Reaſon* for the *Change :* Which is tacitly admitting they could not produce the firſt ; and if call'd
upon for the laſt, 'tis thought they would be at
ſome Loſs to find it ; there being ſeveral glaring
Abſurdities, not to ſay Contradictions, in this their
critical Emendation.

    1. They leave out the Word ALL in the 2d Line,
which is quite neceſſary here: *Anthonio* taking it
for granted *Ferdinand* is drown'd, by the Contraſt
betwixt the Words *all*, and *ſome*, ſtrengthens his
Project, as it hints a-freſh the Death of the *King's
Son*, which gave Birth to it.

    2. They invalidate the Strength of his Argu-
ment,

ment, as to the End for which *some were cast again*;
viz. *by that Destiny to perform an Act*, (to which,
the mentioning the Death of *Ferdinand*, and the
Marriage of *Claribel*, serves as a Prologue) *i. e.* to
murther *Alonzo*, and seize the Throne: And *Shakespear*, by coupling the *Means* " *being cast again*"
with the *End*, " *by that Destiny to perform*, &c."
shews he meant the Argument to be used conclu-
sively by *Anthonio*, to vanquish the Doubts of *Sebastian*, who appears with great Unaptness to the
Business. But these Gentlemen by putting it in
the *potential Mood*, MAY *by that Destiny*, render it
only probably persuasive; the whole Force of
Anthonio's Reasoning now, being that *by the Destiny
of escaping, they have it in their Power to kill* Alonzo, *and* may *do it if they will*: Whereas *Shakespear*
makes him reason with much more Force; they
are *destin'd* to, and *must* do it.

3. By changing the Preposition *in*, to the
Verb neutral *is*, in the last Line and half, they totally alter the Meaning; contradicting that known
Maxim, that *it is impossible for the same Thing to be,
and not to be at the same Instant*; for if it is *past*, it *is*
not now, and if it *is*, it is not *past*. ALL which Contradictions are avoided, by letting the Passage stand
as it does in the old *Edit*. which wants no Alteration, unless, for the Sake of doing something in
the *Critics* Way, they blot out (as they have) the
Word *that* in the first Hemistich; and if they must
go farther, make the Noun *Destiny*, in the 3d
Line, a Verb, *and by that* destin'd *to perform*, &c.
But these Gentlemen seem to have learnt their
Art from the Professors of a certain Mystery, who
when once call'd in, if they can't find Work, take
Care to make it, though at the Risque of their
Employer's Good, and their own Reputation.

R E-

REMARK XXVII.

Seb. What Stuff is this? How fay you?
'Tis true, my Brother's Daughter's Queen of *Tunis* ;
So is fhe Heir of *Naples :* 'Twixt which Regions
There is *fome Space.*
　　Ant. A *Space*, whofe ev'ry Cubit
Seems to cry out, how fhall that *Claribel*
Meafure (a) us back *by Naples ?* Keep in *Tunis.*
And let *Sebaftian* wake. ―――――

(a) *Meafure us back* by *Naples ?*] This Paffage is
now alter'd thus ;

　　――――― *how fhall that* Claribel
Meafure us back to *Naples ? Keep in* Tunis,
And let Sebaftian *wake.* ――― ―――

But furely with great Injuftice to the Author's
poetical Imagination ; which, as it animates each
Cubit to *cry out*, fo, it makes *Naples* the Inftrument of Menfuration, and not like them, barely
the *Ratio* of Diftance: For Ships, Seas, and Winds,
were equally capable of carrying her back from
Tunis to *Naples*, as they had been of bringing her
from *Naples* to *Tunis* ; and therefore not the *Means*
but the *Motive* of her returning, is here enquired
after by ʜᴏᴡ, and the Place poetically put for
the Bufinefs.

But thofe clear-fighted Gentlemen, Meffieurs
Theob. and *Warb.* not being able to conceive why
Claribel fhould go beyond *Naples*; that being the
only Senfe they could perceive in the Word ʙʏ,
(tho' if they had remember'd their old Friend
William Lilly, they might have recollected it ferv-
ed

ed for a Sign to the Ablative, as well as for a Prepofition to the Accufative Cafe) they concluded it wrong, and therefore cafhier'd it; and with it as bold an Image, as perhaps any in *Shakefpear*.

By the Change of Pointing they have alfo loft another Beauty,

—— *keep in* Tunis,
And let Sebaftian *wake*. ——

as they read it, conveying no Idea at all, as fhe cannot meafure the Cubits, (as they would have her) back TO *Naples*, and keep in *Tunis* too : But if it ftands as above quoted, from the old *Edit.* (or if they do not like a Period, let them put a Colon there) it will appear a beautiful Apoftrophe to *Claribel*, advifing her to remain fafe and quiet where fhe is, and not attempt the Danger and Difficulty of the Voyage, as fhe will have not only the Winds and Waves to encounter in her Paffage, but alfo the Traitor's Power, when fhe arrives. *Anthonio* then directly returns to his Purpofe, and calls upon *Sebaftian* to be attentive :

And let Sebaftian wake.

Thus in *Julius Cæfar*,

—————— *O Confpiracy !*
Sham'ft thou to fhew thy dang'rous Brow by Night,
When Evils are moft free ! O then, by Day,
Where wilt thou find a Cavern dark enough,
To mafque thy monft'rous Vifage ? Seek none Confpiracy.

R E-

REMARK XXVIII.

Seb. But for your Confcience.

Ant. (b) I, Sir, where lies that? if 'twere a Kybe,
'Twou'd put me to my Slipper: But I feel not
This Deity in my Bofom; *twenty* Confciences
That ftand 'twixt me and *Milan,* candy'd be they
And melt e'er they moleft. Here lies your Brother,
No better than the Earth he lies upon, *&c.*

(b) *I, Sir, where lies that?*] The modern Editors
have varied this Paffage, by dividing the Lines
thus,

> Seb. *But for your Confcience.*
> Ant. *I, Sir, where lies that?*
> *If 'twere a Kybe, 'twould put me to my Slipper:*
> *But I feel not this Deity in my Bofom.*
> Ten *Confciences that ftand 'twixt me and* Milan,
> *Candy'd be they and melt e'er they moleft!*
> *Here lies your Brother* ———
> *No better than the Earth he lies upon,* &c.

and altered the Poet's Word *Twenty* to *Ten,* for the
Sake of Metre, 'tis to be fuppofed, but fhew no
Authority for thus difturbing the old Text; and
however the Meafure may be permitted to pafs,
there appears no Reafon why they fhould leffen the
Force of the Poet's Expreffion full half; nor is
Mr. *Warb.*'s Explanation of the Term *candy'd, p.*39.
n. 4. " i. e. *did ten Confciences play all their Tricks*
" *with me, fometimes proving very ftubborn, and fome-*
" *times again as fupple; now frozen up with Cold,*
" *now diffolved with Heat; yet they fhould ne'er* mo-
" left, *&c."* quite fatisfactory; the Poet feeming
here to allude to the common Effect of Things fo
pre-

preferv'd, and makes *Anthonio* declare all the Re-
morfes of his Confcience, which he happily ex-
preffes by *twenty Confciences*, fhall as eafily melt as
a candy'd Sweatmeat, and give him no more
Trouble.

The Break made by them at the End of the 6th
Line, which is not in the Edition of 1632, has no
Force, nay, is ufelefs where they have placed it;
for if a Paufe is at all neceffary, it ought to be
made after the next Line,

—— here lies your Brother,
No better than the Earth he lies upon ; ——

where it will be much more natural between the
Defcription of the State *Alonfo* is in, Sleep; and
that *Anthonio* propofes to put him in, Death.

REMARK XXIX.

Ant. This antient (c) *Morfel*, this Sir Prudence, who
Shou'd not ubpraid our Courfe. ——

(c) *This ancient* Morfel] This Term *Morfel*, Mr.
Warb. p. 40. *n.* 5. is very angry with, and fays we
muft read *Moral*, and has accordingly alter'd the
Text, faying, 'tis a Way of Speaking very fami-
liar with *Shakefpear*, and cites for Proof,

And why, my Lady Wifdom, *hold your Tongue, good* Prudence. Rom. & Jul. Act iii. Sc. ult.

which gives no Strength to his Affertion ; for tho'
Morality is true Wifdom, yet there have been, who
chofe to be held for wife Men, who were not over-
burthened with Morals, as this Editor may find in

a

a very wife and chriftian Note, on the Speech of
Wolfey, in HEN. VIII. ACT 3. Sc. *ult.* where it is
faid, " *a good Chriftian*," will make a very *ill*, and
unjuft Statefman.   The Poet's Defign here was to
fhew in what great Contempt *Anthonio* held all
Appearance of Goodnefs, and not to make him
give *Gonzalo* the Eulogium, juftly due to his real
Character; wherefore, he treats him in that diminutive Manner, which is common with this Author;
as *Hamlet* fays,

  A King of Shreds *and* Patches.   Act iii. Sc. 14.

And in another Place,

  Ham. *The King,* is a Thing. ——
  Guild. A Thing, *my Lord?*
  Ham. *Of* nothing. —— HAM. ACT iv. *Sc.* 4.

Which are exactly equivalent to *Morfel* here, and
ufed to fhew the higheft Contempt in the Speaker.

REMARK XXX.

Enter Ariel *with Mufic and Song.*
 Ar. My Mafter, thro' his Art, forefees the Danger,
That you (his Friend) are in; and fends me forth
(For elfe his Project dies) (d) to keep *them* living.

(d) *To keep* them *living*] Mr. *Warb. p.* 40. *n.* 6
fays *Alonfo* and *Anthonio* are the Perfons meant by
them, above, and reafons very drolly on the Alteration made by the *Oxford Editor*, who changes
them into *you:* But it will be fomething difficult for
this Gentleman to fhew, how *Profpero*'s Project at
all depended upon *Anthonio*'s Life, or that *that* was
in

in any Sort of Danger since coming to Land; for
however strong his Intention was to murder *Alonso*
and *Gonzalo*, he says not one Word of *Suicide*, nor
does he betray the least Apprehension of Harm
from *Sebastian* or the others, who are asleep or ab-
sent; it is therefore clear, the Persons to be kept
living, were only those who were in Danger of
dying, *Alonso*, as necessary to *Prospero's* Project,
and *Gonzalo* as his Friend.

REMARK XXXI.

Gon. Now, good Angels, preserve the King!
[*They wake.*

Alon. Why, how now, ho? Awake? Why are you
    drawn?
Wherefore this ghastly Looking?

Gon. What's the Matter?

Seb. While we stood here securing your Repose,
Even now, *we heard a hollow Burst of bellowing*
Like Bulls, or rather Lions; did't not wake you?
It struck mine Ear most horribly.

Alon. I heard nothing.

Ant. O, 'twas a Din, to fright a Monster's Ear;
To make an Earthquake: Sure, it was the Roar
Of a whole Herd of Lions.

Alon. Heard you this?

Gon. Upon my Honour, Sir, I heard a Humming,
And that a strange one too, (e) *which did awake me.*

(e) *Which did awake me.*] The Air of Probability
here given to *Sebastian's* and *Anthonio's* Pretence of
having heard a violent Noise, which had occasion'd
them to draw their Weapons, by the Confirmation
of *Gonzalo*, who had really been wak'd by *Ariel's*
Sing-

Singing in his Ear, is a fhining Proof of the Poet's
great Skill and Judgment.

REMARK XXXII.

Enter Stephano *finging.*
Cal. Do not torment me. Oh !
Ste. What's the Matter ? (f) Have we Devils here ?
Do you put Tricks upon's with *Salvages* and *Men of
Inde ?*

(f) *Have we Devils here ?*] This feems to be much
more a Sneer at fome particular Fraud, ufed in the
Author's Time, by fhewing fomething fictitious
under thofe Titles, than at the Travels of *Maundeville ;* for as to his *State of Devils,* mentioned by
Mr. *Warb. p.* 44. *n.* 9. it muft appear a great Sole-
cifm in the Poet to fatirize the Hiftorian, for that,
when his whole Play is built on the Doctrine of
their Inhabiting the Earth, and doing whatever
Mifchief, their Mafters, the Enchanters, fet them
upon.

REMARK XXXIII.

Ste. ⸺ (g) his *forward Voice* now, is to fpeak well
of his Friends, his *backward Voice* is to *utter* foul Speeches
and to detract.

(g) *His forward Voice*] Mr. *Warb. p.* 45. has
chang'd *utter* in this Speech for *fpatter,* againft all
Authority, as well as Reafon, Senfe, and Grammar;
for to make a Voice fpatter [*commaculare, refpergere*]
foul Speeches, is perhaps a greater (7) " *Anomaly,*"
than any in *Shakefpear,* and *mixing Modes* with a Ven-

(7) *Warb.* Preface, *p.* 16.

geance :

geance: He has indeed mark'd this Paſſage as a Beauty, as it certainly is, being an elegant deſcriptive Satire, on all time-ſerving Flatterers, who ſpeak fair to the Faces of thoſe they hang upon, but behind their Backs traduce and revile them. That this Vice was frequently practiſed in thoſe Times, many Paſſages, in our Author, and *Ben. Johnſon,* will make apparent. Mr. *Theob.*'s Conjecture, that *Butler* took the Hint of his Deſcription of. Fame from this Paſſage, is far from unreaſonable.

REMARK XXXIV.

Ste. —— How cam'ſt thou to be the (h) *Siege* of this (i) *Moon-Calf?* Can he (k) *vent Trinculo's?*

(h) The *Siege,* &c.] An Alluſion to an Effect of Medicine.

(i) *This* Moon-Calf?] Mr. *Warb. p.* 45. *n.* 1. has given a metaphyſical Account of the Uſe of this Term, but if he had conſidered it phyſically he might have found it was originally appropriated to a monſtrous, or unform'd Production, called in Latin *Mola, Partus-Lunaris,* [a *Lump, Mole,* or *Moon-Birth*] in which Senſe *Shakeſpear* very properly uſes it to his Monſter.

(k) *Can he* vent *Trinculo's*] The Alluſion to Medicine continued.

REMARK XXXV.

Trin. —— this is a very ſhallow Monſter ; (l) *I afraid of him?*

(l) *I afraid of Him?*] Meſſrs. *Theob. p.* 38. *n.* 18. and *Warb. p.* 46. *n.* 2. ſay this is a Brag of *Trinculo's,* which it is very far from ; it being a direct

Ac-

Acknowledgment that he had been so, and now is angry with himself for it, being conscious it had been discovered by *Caliban*; and hence arises the Contempt *Caliban* ever after has for *Trinculo*, and the Regard for *Stephano*'s Courage, which is often in his Mouth, and which without this Preparation would have been quite unnatural.

REMARK XXXVI.

Cal. I prythee, let me bring thee where Crabs grow ;
And I, with my long Nails, will dig thee Pig-nuts ;
Shew thee a Jay's Nest; and instruct thee how
To snare the nimble Marmazet ; I'll bring thee
To clust'ring Filberts; and sometimes I'll get thee
(m) *Young Scamels* from the Rocks. ———

(m) *Young Scamels*] Mr. *Theob. p.* 39. *n.* 19. alters this to *young Shamois*, and assigns several Reasons for his Alteration ; and Mr. *Warb. p.* 47. *n.* 3. confirms the Change, *ex Cathedra*, with a magisterial Authority ; " We should read *Shamois*, i. e. young " Kids." But notwithstanding the Sentiments of the one, and the peremptory Decree of the other, of these Gentlemen, it may be asked why we should read so ? *Caliban* is no where in the Play fam'd for Swiftness, but frequently accused of Sloth, and here pretends to nothing but what may be done at great Leisure :

——— *bring thee where Crabs grow* ;
——— *dig thee Pig-nuts* ;
Shew thee a Jay's Nest; *and instruct thee how*
To snare the nimble Marmazet; *I'll bring thee*
To clust'ring Filberts, and sometimes I'll get thee
Young Scamels from the Rocks.

there

therefore *Shamois* cannot be right, their Celerity
being remarkable, even to a Standard for Swift-
nefs: But then either fomething muft be found,
that the Name *Scamels*, and the particular Situation
here pointed out will fuit, or elfe we muft read
with Mr. *Theob. Seamel*, for *Sea-gull*, a Bird that
builds amongft Rocks, from whence the young
ones might be taken; and fuppofe that in tranfcribing, or at the Prefs, the [E] was chang'd into a [c]. But the Shell-Fifh called the Limpet,
(whofe Shell is generally known by the Name of
the nipple Shell) are called in fome Countries SCAMS;
they are found on the Rocks, and are by many rec-
koned delicious Food; and from thefe, *Shakefpear*
might take the Liberty to form a Diminutive, and
make his Word SCAMELS.

REMARK XXXVII.

ACT III. Sc. I.

Enter Ferdinand *bearing a Log.*

Ferd. There be fome Sports are painful, but their
Labour
Delight in them fets off; fome Kinds of Bafenefs
Are nobly undergone; and moft poor Matters
Point to rich Ends. This my mean Tafk wou'd be
As heavy to me, as 'tis odious; but
The Miftrefs which I ferve, quickens what's dead
And makes my Labours Pleafures: O fhe is
Ten Times more gentle than her Father's crabbed;
And he's compos'd of Harfhnefs. I muft move
Some Thoufands of thefe Logs, and pile them up,
Upon a fore Injunction. My fweet Miftrefs
Weeps, when fhe fees me work, and fays fuch Bafenefs,

Had

Had ne'er like Executer : I forget ;
But thefe fweet Thoughts do ev'n refrefh my Labour
Moft bufy leaft when I do it.

(n) *Moft bufy leaft* when I do it] This the Commentators (*Theob. p.* 41. *n.* 20. *Warb. p.* 48. *l.* ult.)
have chang'd to *bufy-lefs*, but with what Appearance
of Reafon or Sentiment lies on them to fhew ; for
if *Ferdinand* was bufy-lefs in his Labour, *i. e.* if his
Work confifted in doing nothing, he ftood in no
need of thofe fweet Thoughts to refrefh him under
the Preffure ; and if his Thoughts were bufy-lefs,
during his Labour, they contributed nothing to
his Refrefhment; fo that let them make their *Bufy-lefs* an Adjective to either *Thoughts* or *Labour*, and
to one of them it muft be, or it is ufelefs in the
Sentence, it conveys no clearer Idea than the old
Reading. But why may not this Paffage be re-
folved into that (8) hard Conftruction Mr. *Warb.*
fpeaks of, and be underftood thus ; *But thefe fweet*
leaft *Thoughts [of* Miranda *his Miftrefs] do even refrefh my* moft bufy Labour, *when I do it.* Though
'tis not impoffible but the Original was a double
Superlative, which was no uncommon Mode of
Expreffion in thofe Days, and then it may ftand
thus :

But thefe fweet Thoughts *do ev'n refrefh my Labour,*
Moft bufieft *when I do it.*

which may fignify either, thofe Thoughts being
moft bufy, when he is at Work, or that they refrefh
his *bufieft* or greateft Labour when he does it.

(8) Preface to *Warb.* Edit. *p.* 16. § 2.

RE-

REMARK XXXVIII.

Mir. —— (o) Hence, *bashful Cunning*,
And prompt me plain, and holy Innocence.
I am your Wife, if you will marry me,
If not, I'll die your Maid : to be your Fellow,
You may deny me ; but I'll be your Servant
Whether you will or no.

(o) *Hence,* bashful Cunning] The noble Simplicity
of this Addrefs, is as beautiful as any Thing in
Shakefpear's Works. Mr. *Prior*, in his *Henry* and
Emma, feems to have his Eye on this Speech in thefe
Lines.

This potent Beauty, this triumphant Fair,
This happy Object of our different Care,
Her let me follow ; her let me attend,
A Servant : (*She may fcorn the Name of Friend.*)

REMARK XXXIX.

SCENE II.

Cal. Yea, yea, my Lord, I'll yield him thee afleep,
Where thou may'ft knock a Nail into his Head.
Ar. Thou lieft, thou can'ft not.
Cal. What a pied Ninny's this ? thou fcurvy Patch !
I do befeech thy Greatnefs give him Blows,
And take his Bottle from him ; when that's gone,
He fhall drink nought but Brine, for I'll not fhew him
Where the quick Frefhes are.
Step. *Trinculo*, run into no further Danger, interrupt
the Monfter one Word, *farther !* and by this Hand, I'll
turn my Mercy out of Doors, and make a Stock-Fifh of
thee.

Trin.

Trin. Why what did I ? I did nothing ; (p) *I'll go no
further off.*

(p) *I'll go* no *further off*] *Caliban* is propoſing
the Plot to murder *Proſpero*, to *Stephano* and *Trin-
culo*, who are both drunk ; *Ariel*, ſuppoſed inviſi-
ble, interrupts him, which Interruption he imputes
to *Trinculo* ; whereupon *Stephano* quarrels with *Trin-
culo*, and threatens to beat him, on which *Trinculo*
inſiſts he has done nothing, and refuſes to go far-
ther from them : But Mr. *Theob. p.* 46. and Mr.
Warb. p. 54. (probably following Mr. *Pope*) have
expung'd the Negative, and thereby defaced the
ſtrong Features of Nature, here mark'd by the Poet,
who all through the Character draws *Trinculo* a con-
ſcious Coward, and continually endeavouring to
hide his Fear, by Pretences to Bravery, though in
vain ; for even *Caliban* has found him out, and in
this Scene tells him ſo more than once :

I'll not ſerve him, he is not valiant.

I wou'd my valiant *Maſter wou'd deſtroy thee.*

———— *If thy Greatneſs will
* Revenge *it on him, for I know* thou dar'ſt,
But this Thing dares not ————

Beat him *enough, after a little Time,*
I'll beat him too.

The Humour of the Scene is greatly heightened
by *Ariel's* being ſuppoſed inaudible, as well as in-
viſible to *Trinculo*, whoſe Curioſity to hear *Caliban's*
Plot, occaſions the Refuſal to go any farther from
him and *Stephano*, till the latter, by an actual Beat-
ing obliges him to ſhift his Ground : And there is
little Room to doubt but this Speech was originally
ſpoke as above pointed, or elſe *Stephano*, to his
firſt

firft Threats, added fome Sign or Motion for *Trinculo*, to remove to fome farther Diftance, to either of which his affected Refolution not to ftir, was a proper and pertinent Anfwer. Whoever has read this Poet attentively, will find many Examples of this abrupt Manner of Addrefs, as to *Ferdinand* and *Miranda* afterwards in this Play.

> *Ter. Mir.* We wifh you Peace.
> *Prof.* Come with a Thought; *I thank you: Ariel*, come.

Where he calls firft on *Ariel*, and then abruptly breaks that Call, to thank them for their kind Wifhes, and then again calls his Spirit.

REMARK XL.

SCENE IV.

> *Seb.* —— Now I will believe
> That there are Unicorns: That in *Arabia*
> There is one Tree, the Phœnix Throne; one Phœnix
> At this Hour reigning there.
> *Ant.* I'll believe both;
> And what does elfe want Credit, come to me,
> And I'll be fworn 'tis true: (q) *Travellers* ne'er did lie,
> Tho' Fools at home condemn them.

(q) Travellers *ne'er did lie*] This Paffage is a fine Compliment to Sir *Walter Raleigh*, who publifhed his Travels towards the latter End of Queen *Elizabeth*'s Reign, and in them fupported the Credit of *Maundeville* in feveral Inftances, wherein before he ftood charged with Falfhood, of which *Shakefpear* finely takes Notice in thefe Lines:

> —— *When we were Boys,*
> *Who'd* believe *that there were* Mountaineers,
> Dew-lapt like Bulls, whofe Throats had hanging at 'em
>   Wallets

Wallets of Flesh? or that there were such Men,
Whose Heads stood in their Breasts? *which now, we*
    find
Each putter out (r) of *five for one, will bring us*
Good *Warrant of.*

These Passages also negatively fix the Date of
this Play, that it was not wrote before 1596 or 97;
for though Sir *Martin Frobisher*, Sir *Francis Drake*,
Sir *Walter Raleigh*, and Captain *Davis*, had made
several Voyages between 1576 and 1586, yet Sir
Walter did not publish his Travels, till after his first
Voyage to *Guiana*, which was not made till 1595;
and there is great Reason to believe it was not wrote
till long after that, *viz.* till 1612, or 13, or at
earliest, not till 1610, as has been observed in the
Introduction; and this will appear more probable,
if it is considered that *Ben. Johnson*, in the Introduction to his (9) *Bartholomew Fair*, after having had
a Fling at *Shakespear*'s *Titus Andronicus*, as an old
Play, (it making its Appearance, according to him,
about 1589; *Shakespear* then being not more than
Twenty-five Years old) speaks of his *Winter's Tale*,
and this Play, as recent Performances. *Ben.* in
that Piece, satirizes several other of *Shakespear*'s
Plays, as the *Merry Wives* of *Windsor*, *Much ado
about Nothing*, *Love's Labour lost*, and the *Midsum-
mer Night's Dream.*

(r) *Each putter out* of *five for one*] Mr. *Theob. p.*
50. *n.* 22. and Mr. *Warb. p.* 58. *n.* 5. have alter'd this
Line to

Each putter out on *five for one.*

Which may be admitted, as it does no Injury to
the Sense or Satire of the Poet, who undoubtedly

(9) *Bartholomew Fair* was first play'd in 1614.

alluded

alluded to the Method of Infurance, common in
his Time, as Mr. *Theob. (ubi fupra)* has fhewn clearly from a fimilar Paffage in *Ben. Johnfon's Every
Man out of his Humour.*

REMARK XLI.

SCENE IV.

Ar. You are three Men of Sin, whom Deftiny
That hath to Inftrument this lower World,
And what is in't : The never-furfeited Sea,
(s) Hath caus'd to belch up *you*;

(s) *Hath caus'd to belch up* you] Mr. *Theob. p.* 51.
n. 23. has rightly ftruck out *you* here, it being evidently an Error of the Prefs ; and is therein followed by the later Editions, though without making
him any Acknowledgment ; but it is fubmitted,
whether their Pointing (that of the *Fol.* 1632, being
evidently wrong) may not be amended ? The modern ones point this Paffage thus :

You are three Men of Sin whom Deftiny
(That hath to Inftrument this lower World,
And what is in't) *the never furfeited Sea
Hath caus'd to belch up* ; —————

by which they feem to confine the Operation of
Deftiny to fublunary Things only, when it is poffible, and even more than probable, the Poet did
not intend to limit her Sphere of Action, but to
fhew what *Inftruments*, or Means fhe acted by ; his
Senfe being clearly, *You are three Men of Sin*, [for
finful Men] *whom Deftiny, that hath this lower World,
and what is in't to* [for] *Inftrument, hath caufed the never furfeited Sea to belch up* ; which Senfe, perhaps,
will appear ftronger, if the Paffage is thus pointed:
You

You are three Men of Sin, whom Deſtiny;
That hath to Inſtrument, this lower World
And what is in't, the never-ſurfeited Sea
Hath caus'd to belch up : ——

This whole Speech of *Ariel's* is beautifully imagined, to ſet the Senſe of their Guilt in ſuch a
glaring Light, as to awaken their Remorſe ; (which
all their Sufferings had not been able to do) and
to point out the only Means of Relief,

—— *Hearts Sorrow,*
And a clear Life enſuing. ——

Theſe moral Strokes, which abound in *Shakeſpear,*
prove him a good Man, as well as a great Poet.

Remark XLII.

Gon. All three of them are deſperate ; their great
Guilt,
(t) Like Poiſon, given to work *a long Time after,*
Now gin's to bite the Spirits.

(t) *Like Poiſon, given to work* a long Time after]
This beautiful and apt Simile, contains in it a Piece
of Marine Tradition ; the Seamen being ſtrongly
perſuaded that the *Africans,* eſpecially on the *Guiney
Coaſt,* can temper Poiſon ſo, as to operate at any
preciſe Time, and in any limited Degree, and that
during the Interval between taking and operating,
the Patient ſhall feel no Manner of Effect from the
Doſe.

REMARK XLIII.

ACT IV. Sc. 1.

Prof. If I have too austerely punish'd you,
Your Compensation, makes Amends ; for I
Have given you here, (u) *a Third* of my own Life;
Or that for which I live.

(u) *Have given you here* a Third *of my own Life.*]
Mr. *Theob. p.* 53. *n.* 24. changes this to a *Thread* ; and
Mr. *Warb. p.* 61. adopts, and *n. a.* acknowledges
whence he had it; (a Condescension not common
with this Gentleman.) But the old Reading may
be left in Repose : *A Third,* being some certain
proportional Part of what was dear and valuable to
him, and which he could share with another; but
query, if *Prospero* parted with the *Thread,* i. e. the
Whole of his Life, Life itself, whether he could
with any Propriety be said still to live, as in the next
Line he is made to do ? And the Instances produced
by Mr. *Theob.*

And let not Bardolfe's vital Thread *be cut.*　　HEN. V.

His Thread of Life *had not so soon decay'd.* 1st Pt. HEN.vi.

Argo *their* Thread of Life *is spun.*　　2d Pt. HEN. vi.

———— *shore his old* Thread *in Twain.*　　OTHEL.

instead of supporting his Alteration of this Passage,
prove that *Shakespear* constantly used *Thread of
Life,* in the strict poetick Sense, for Life, not for
any Part or Portion of it, for that *by,* and not that
for, which (as it is here expressed) any one liv'd ;
and though he found that *Prospero* had no Wife living ; nor any other Child but *Miranda* ; and that
　　　　　　　　　　　　　　　　　Dimi-

Dimidium Animæ meæ cannot be conftrued into three
Halves ; yet, if he had recollected *the Occafion* of
this Speech ; and *to whom* the Speech was fpoken ;
and *how many* interefted in the Speech were prefent,
at the fpeaking ; he might have thought perhaps,
the introducing fuch a Son-in-Law into *Profpero*'s
Family, who fettled a Remainder Expectant of a
Crown upon his Daughter ; and delivering him from
Wretchednefs and Banifhment, reftored him to
Power, and princely Grandeur ; might tempt the
Old Gentleman to imagine his Satisfaction was in-
creafed one full Third : And in the Height of that
Imagination, he might be induc'd, by a poetic Li-
cence, to exprefs himfelf fo, as to be clearly underftood, by an ordinary Reader, to have fuch an
Efteem for the Perfon, to whom he was then giv-
ing an only Daughter he doated on, as to reckon
him abfolutely as one of his own Family, and an
effential *third* Part of his future Happinefs, though
fuch an Expreffion tranfgreffed against the *fevere
Canons of literal Criticifm.* And it is fomething
ftrange, Mr. *Warb.* fhould fo haftily adopt this Alteration, as he has prov'd in his Dedication, to his
Edit. he has no private Reafons of his own, why a
Son-in-Law fhould not be fo regarded.

REMARK XLIV.

Prof. Then as my (10) *Gift,* and thine own Acqui-
fition,
Worthily purchas'd, take my Daughter.
If thou doft break her Virgin Knot, before
All fanctimonious Ceremonies may

(10) The Folio Edition 1632 reads *Gueft* here for *Gift,* which
is properly reftored by the more modern Editions ; and thefe, and
thefe only, were the Emendations neceffary.

With

With full, and holy Rite be minifter'd,
(w) No fweet Afperfions fhall the Heav'ns let fall
To make this Contract grow : But *barren Hate*,
Sour-ey'd Difdain, *and Difcord*, fhall beftrew
The Union of your Bed, with Weeds fo loathly,
That you fhall hate it both : Therefore take heed,
As *Hymen*'s Lamps fhall light you.

 Fer. As I hope,
For quiet Days, fair Iffue, and long Life,
With fuch Love as 'tis now ; the murkieft Den,
The moft opportune Place, the ftrong'ft Suggeftion
Our worfer Genius can, fhall never melt
Mine Honour into Luft, to take away
The Edge of that Day's Celebration,
When I fhall think, or *Phœbus*' Steeds are founder'd,
Or Night kept chain'd below.

 Pro. Fairly fpoke :
Sit then and talk with her : She is thine own, *&c*.

(w) *No fweet Afperfions*, &c.] Though the beautiful Sentiments, and fine Imagery, in thefe Speeches, are a fufficient Excufe for tranfcribing them, yet the chief Motive was, becaufe on this Paffage is founded the Conjecture, that the following Mafque was intended, by the Poet, as a Compliment to the young Earl of *Effex*, on his Contract of Marriage with the Lady *Frances Howard*, and may fix the Date of this Play to the Year 1614 ; when the fad Train of Mifchiefs fo artfully, and finely enumerated here, fell to that Nobleman's Lot: And fhews the fkilful Addrefs of the Author, to clear JAMES I. (who, 'tis well known, was by much too bufy in the Divorce which followed) from Odium ; by infinuating 'twas fomething done by the Earl himfelf, to which the Evil brought on him was owing. And this Conjecture feems to be ftrengthened by the following Speeches in the next Scene.

         Pro.

(68)

Pro. *Look thou be true ; do not give Dalliance*
Too much the Rein ; the strongest Oaths are Straw
To th' Fire i'th' Blood : Be more abstemious,
Or else, good Night your Vow.
    Fer. *I warrant you, Sir :*
The white, cold Virgin Snow *upon my Heart,*
Abates *the* Ardour *of my Liver.*

A Situation, the Earl admitted he found himself
in with Respect to his Countess; (though not so to
other Women) and that supposed to be the Effect
of *Forman*'s magical Medicines.

REMARK XLV.

SCENE III.

A MASQUE. Enter *Iris.*

Ir. *Ceres*, most bounteous Lady, (11) thy rich Leas
Of Wheat, Rye, Barley, Oats, and Pease;
Thy turfy Mountains, where live nibbling Sheep,
And flat Meads thatch'd with (x) *Stover*, them to keep ;
Thy Banks, with (y) *pioned*, and *twilled* Brims,
Which spungy *April*, at thy Hest, betrims
To make cold Nymphs chaste Crowns ; and thy (z)
        Broom-Groves,
Whose Shadow the dismissed Batchelor loves,
Being Love-lorn ; thy (a) *Pole-clipt* Vineyard,
And thy Sea-marge steril, and rocky-hard,
Where thou thy self dost Air ; the Queen o'th'
        Sky,
Whose wat'ry Arch, and Messenger am I,
Bids thee leave these ; and with her sovereign Grace,
Here on this Grass-plot, in this very Place,
To come and sport ;

(11) The Edit. 1632, reads *the* rich Leas.

(x)

(

(69)

(x) —— *with* Stover *them to keep*] Stover is a Contraction of *Eftover*, an old Law Word, fignifying an Allowance for Maintenance in Food, and Nourifhment, or for Repairs.

(y) Thy *pioned* and *twilled* Brims] Mr. *Theob. p.* 55. changes *twilled* to *tulip'd*, and Mr. *Warb. p.* 63. follows him, but neither of them take any Notice of the Alteration. Tis true, here is evidently an Error, but as true, only an Error of the Prefs; which is eafily rectified by throwing out the [*w*], and reading *tilled*; but thefe Gentlemen fubftituted *tulip'd* from mifunderftanding the Word *pioned* before it, which they, as is clear by their Alteration, underftood of the *Pæony*, or *Piony*, a Flower; when the Poet meant only to fhew the Fertility of the Banks of Rivers, and the Caufe of that Fertility, there being *pioned*, i. e. trench'd or dug; and *tilled* or manured; in Oppofition to the Barrennefs of the Sea-Shore, which he a little after calls *Sea-marge*, fteril, and rocky-hard.

The Orthography will juftify this Reading; for however ignorant the *Theatrical* or *Poetical* Editors might be, it is not to be fuppofed the very learned Mr. *Warb.* could be at a Lofs how to form an *Englifh* Participle from *Pæonia*, or that, if the Flower had been intended by the Poet, there muft have been a [*y*] with an Apoftrophe, thus,

—— *Thy* piony'd *and* tulip'd Brims, *&c.*

which as there is not, 'tis plain, thefe Flowers were not in the Author's Mind, though he fpeaks of thofe

To make cold Nymphs chafte Crowns;

produced by *fpungy* April, at the Command of *Ceres*, to trim the River Banks; which any Reader
may

may fee means the fpontaneous Productions of the
Spring, in a good Soil, well cultivated. And wherever he has deck'd his Perfonages with Flowers, he
has preferred the wild Glories of the Field, to the
more cultured Beauties of the Garden, as may be
feen, in *As you like it*, *Lear*, and *Hamlet*.

(z) *and thy broom Groves*,] The *Oxford Edit*. having altered this to *brown Groves*, Mr. *Warb*. p. 63.
n. a. adopts it, and for once pays his Tribute of
Acknowledgment to that Editor; but the Reading
of the old Editions ought to ftand, on the Authority of all the Copies, and as conveying the fimp-
ler Image.

(a) *thy* pole-clipt *Vineyard*] This Mr. *Warb*. p.
63. *n.* 6. alters to *pale-clipt*, which (however juft
his Animadverfions, on Mr. *Gildon's* Expofition
may be) cannot be right: For though the learned
Gentleman may have no Conception of any other
Vineyards than thofe he has feen in his own native
Climate, where PALING is frequently made ufe of,
Shakefpear had a more extenfive Idea, and a clearer
Knowledge ; and it may be affirm'd, never thought
of fencing them with *Pales*, a Kind of Inclofure
not ufed, fcarcely known, in the Countries famous
for Vineyards: And the old Reading is righteft;
the Poles, (and not the Vines, or Vineyard) being
clipt or twin'd round, and here ufed, to fhew the
Author meant a Vineyard, properly fo called, and
not *efpalier*, or Wall-Vines.

It may be faid, that poffibly Mr. *Warb*. had his
Eye on the Defcription of *Achilles's* Shield in the
18th. Iliad, which if admitted, will only prove
that *Shakefpear* underftood the Original better, than
his Editor. The Paffage alluded to is this,

E'5

E'ν δ' ετιθϊ ϛαφυλησι βριθουσαν αλοην,
Καλην, χρυσειην, μελανες δ'ανα βοτρυες ησαν'
E'ϛηκει δε καμαξι διαμπερες αργυρεησιν.
Αμφι δε, χυανεην, καπετον, περι δ' ερκος ελαϲϲε. σϲ|
Καϲϲιτερου. Καϲϲιτερου

In eo etiam pofuit uvis valde oneratam vineam,
Pulchram, Auream, nigri autem per eam racemi erant
Stabat *vero* palis SUFFULTA *per totum* Argenteis,
Circum a cœruleam foffam. *Circa etiam* fepem *duxit*
Ex ftanno. ———— ————

A loaded Vineyard grac'd the ample round;
(12) To filver Poles, *the fruitful* Vines *were bound.*
Wrought fair in Gold, the black, ripe Clufters fhone:
A Ditch *cœrulean round the Area run;*
Fenc'd with a Hedge *of Tin.* ————

By which any one may fee *Homer* made no Ufe of
Pales, but inclofed his Vineyard, with a Hedge and
Ditch: *Kamax* and *Palus* are interpreted *a Pole, or*
Prop for a Vine, and *Suffulta,* [underpropt or fup-
ported] in the *Latin* Verfion, fufficiently proves
what were intended by *Palis Argenteis.*

REMARK XLVI.

JUNO *fings.*

Honour, Riches, marriage Bleffing,
Long Continuance, and Increafing,
Hourly Joys be ftill upon you;
(b) *Juno* fings her Bleffings on you:
Earth's Increafe, and foyfon-Plenty,
Barns and Garners never empty;

(12) The 2d and 3d Lines are here tranfpofed.

Vines,

Vines, with cluft'ring Bunches growing,
Plants, with goodly Burthen bowing ;
Spring come to you, at the fartheft,
In the very End of Harveft :
Scarcity and Want fhall fhun you,
Ceres Bleffing fo is on you.

(b) Juno *fings her Bleffings on you.*] This Song,
which all the former Editions give entirely to *Juno*,
Mr. *Theob. p. 56. n.* 25. has divided, giving her but
the four firft Lines, and the remaining eight to
Ceres; his Reafons for which, any one may fee in
the Place above-cited: And this Divifion Mr.
Warb. p. 65. embraces, though, (according to his
general Cuftom) without any Acknowledgment.
And admitting this Divifion to be right, and the
Poets original Intention, the Author might have
his Reafons, as well as the Player Editors, for giving the whole to *Juno* in the Performance, *viz.* the
having but one Voice that could execute it ; and
that this was the Cafe, feems to be confirm'd by the
joint Confent of all the elder Editions: It being
well known, or at leaft admitted, that they all had
near the fame Authority, *i. e.* the Reprefentation,
or the Stage Copies. For though in fome of the
Titles of the old *Quarto's*, they are faid to be corrected, and enlarged to almoft as much again, the
Materials were probably furnifhed from no other
Storehoufe ; the Author not appearing to have
given himfelf much Trouble, about the Figure his
Offspring made on the outfide of the Theatre.
Therefore 'tis moft reafonable to fuppofe this
whole Sonnet was fung by one Voice, and that in
the Character of *Juno*, and on that Account all
placed to that Character in the feveral printed Copies ; the firft Editors being obliged, for want of
better Guides, to govern themfelves by what they
faw

faw and heard, whether they ftole from the Stage
by Memory, or otherwife, or even printed from
the Stage Copies, with the Confent of the Proprie-
tors, as the Actors then called themfelves, after
Reprefentation. Nor is there fo great a Devia-
tion from Character, in *Juno*'s finging the Whole,
as Mr. *Theob.* feems to infinuate ; for notwithftanding the diftinct Offices affign'd to the two Goddeffes
in poetick Story, yet *Juno*, as Goddefs, and Sym-
bol of the Air, might very properly, and poetically pronounce the Bleffings which *Ceres*, befriended
by her, fhould produce ; and Mr. *Theob.* might as
reafonably infift *Bacchus, Vertumnus, Flora* and *Po-
mona* ought to be introduced on the Scene, to fpeak
their particular Shares of the Benediction ; or fhew
why *Juno*, might not interfere in *Ceres*'s Part, as
fhe does in the Gifts which, according to the Poets,
regularly belong to thofe other Deities.

REMARK XLVII.

Ferd. This is a moft majeftic Vifion, and
(c) Harmonious charmingly : May I be bold
To think thefe Spirits ?

(c) *Harmonious charmingly*] Mr. *Warb. p.* 65. *n.* 7.
calls this Nonfenfe, and by way of cure fubftitutes

Harmonious, charming Lays :

which is a faultier Piece of Grammar, than any
in *Shakefpear* ; as the Author of the Supplement to
Warb. Edition, has fhewn, CANON 8. *p.* 38. and
that ingenious Gentleman, undoubtedly, (if he had
pleafed) could have cleared and fupported the old
Reading,

Reading, notwithstanding the positive Charge of Nonsense, brought against this Passage by Mr. *Warb.* who himself allows, (as has been remarked) (13) *Shakespear*, was very hard in his Construction; and if so, why might it not be supposed, that the Adverb, in this Place, is only plac'd *after*, instead of *before* the Adjective, and wants but to be restor'd to its proper Place?

> This is a most majestic Vision, and
> Charmingly harmonious : ⸺

Will there appear either Incongruity, or false Grammar in such an Alteration? But if *Shakespear*'s Manner be attended to duly, it does not want even this; as the old Reading may be made natural, easy, and very expressive, by barely new pointing the Passage thus,

> *This is a most majestic Vision, and*
> *Harmonious:* charmingly!

A Mode of Expression, when the Mind is strongly agitated with Pleasure, as common, as natural, and shews *Ferdinand* was not content with merely saying it was *harmonious*, without shewing in what Degree (*viz. charmingly*) so.

REMARK XLVIII.

> *Pro.* Spirits which by mine Art,
> I have from (d) *all* their Confines call'd, to enact
> My present Fancies.

(13) Remark XXXVII. P. 58.

(d) *I*

(d) *I have from* all *their Confines call'd*] Mr. *Theob.*
p. 57. *n.* 26. says, " *This* ALL *is obtruded upon us by*
" *the nice Ears of our* modern Editors." And Mr.
Warb. p. 66. as contemptuously as he has, on several Occasions, treated the Judgment of his *quondam*
Friend, and Fellow Critic, implicitly subscribes
here to his Assertion, by expunging the Word out
of his own Edition; and perhaps both those great
Men look on the Edition of 1632 (where that
Word stands) as a very modern one, it not being
quite an hundred Years old, when their joint Labours on this Play were published by Mr. *Theob.*
all whose Authorities, brought to prove *Shakespear*
constantly laid the Accent on the last Syllable of
confine, might have been omitted, except the last,

" *Shipping my self from the Sigæan Shore,*
" *Whence unto these* Confines *my Course I bore.*
PÀRIS to HELEN.

All the rest, reading equally smooth, wherever the
Accent is laid; and one

' *O most potential Love! Vow, Bond, nor Space,*
' *In thee, hath neither Sting, Knot, nor* Confine.

rather requiring the Accent to be laid on the first.

REMARK XLIX.

SCENE IV.

Pro. You look, my Son, in a mov'd Sort,
As if you were dismay'd: Be chearful, Sir;

Our

Our Revels now are ended : Thefe our Actors,
As I foretold you, were all Spirits, and
Are melted into Air, into thin Air ;
(e) And like the bafelefs Fabric of *their Vifion,*
The cloud-capt Towers, the gorgeous Palaces,
The folemn Temples, the great Globe itfelf,
Yea all which it inherit, fhall diffolve ;
And like this infubftantial Pageant faded,
Leave not a Rack behind.

(e) *And like the bafelefs Fabrick of* their Vifion.]
Mr. *Warb. p.* 67. *n.* 8. has much to fay about this
Paffage ; condemning *Shakefpear,* (unlefs his Alteration fhall pafs for *Shakefpear's* Words) for "*wretch-*
"*ed Tautology,* and *aukward Expreffion ;*" and all
to make Way for his imaginary pompous Reading,

And like the bafelefs Fabric of TH' AIR VISIONS :

But does this mend the Matter, admitting it to
want Amendment ? Will the "Veftige of an em-
"bodied Cloud, broken, and diffipated by the
"Wind," prove any folider Bafis, than the thin
Air of which Spirits are faid to be framed ? Or can
a Vifion be faid to be any other than Airy ? The
Term being ftrictly confined to that which has no
Solidity, no Subftance, but merely a Creature of
the Brain, and the Effect of fupernatural Power.
  The "aukward Expreffion" (as this Gentleman
is pleafed to call it) *their Vifion,* is furely ufed here
with great Propriety ; the Spirits who performed
and contrived it, (for any Thing that appears to
the contrary) having the beft Title to have it call'd
theirs. The Tautology, alfo, (mentioned with fuch
                                              Indig-

Indignation) will melt into Air, into thin Air, if
the Speech is divided into its proper Parts;

the bafelefs Fabric *of their Vifion,*

referring to Air, which the Poet had juft before
faid they were compofed of, and returned to; and

———— *this* infubftantial Pageant *faded,*

to the Scene they had juft reprefented, which was
now totally vanifhed ; both finely inculcating, that
all the Power, Wealth, Strength, and Beauty, we
know, morally confidered, is but a Dream, a Vifion,
and like one fhall diffolve, and melt away ; leaving
not fo much as a RACK, or fmalleft Part behind,
to teftify their having ever exifted : As the PSAL-
MIST, with equal Beauty, and greater Strength ex-
preffes it.

Thou haft deftroy'd Cities, *their* Memorial *is* perifh'd
with them. Pf. ix. v. 6.

His Place *cou'd* no where *be found.* Pf. xxxvii. v. 37.

For the Wind paffeth over it, and it is gone, *and the*
Place *thereof fhall* know it no more. Pf. ciii. v. 16.

And that the true Meaning of a *Rack* in this Place,
is, a Fragment, a broken Remnant, the learned
Gentleman himfelf admits by calling it, " *the* Vef-
" tige of *an* EMBODIED CLOUD, broken, *and* dif-
" fipated *by the Wind."* Though what he means
by an " *embody'd Cloud,"* or how the " *Veftige* "
[Footftep, or Trace] of " *a Diffipation* " is to be
difcern'd, is left to himfelf to explain, when he
thinks proper.

REMARK L.

Pro. (f) The Trumpery in my Houfe, go bring it
 hither,
For Stale to catch thefe Thieves.

(f) *The* Trumpery *in my Houfe.*] Mr. *Warb. p.* 70.
n. 2. fays, " If it fhould be afked what Neceffity
" for this Apparatus? I anfwer, that it was the fu-
" perftitious Fancy of the People, in our Author's
" Time, that Witches, Conjurers, &c. had no
" Power over thofe againft whom they would em-
" ploy their Charms, till they had got them at this
" Advantage, committing fome Sin or other, as
" here of Theft." Herein, forgetting on one
Hand, all his own excellent Reafoning (*p.* 69. *n.* 1.)
on the Sin of Ingratitude, and on the other, that
long before, in, and after *Shakefpear*'s Time, the
Power of Witchcraft, was faid to be frequently,
nay, moft commonly exercifed on *Babes* and *Brutes,*
neither of which were extremely liable to be had at
this Advantage, of " *committing fome Sin or other,*"
as being for the moft Part incapable of doing any
Act *Animo Peccandi.* But above all forgetting
that without fome " *Apparatus,* " there would have
been no manifeft Reafon, why the Affaffins fhould
not immediately, on their Appearance, enter the
Cave, and perpetrate their Villany ; which, if they
had, the Stage muft have ftood ftill during that
Time, and which this *Trumpery,* alone, totally prevents, as it diverts them from their main Defign,
and yet keeps the Scene bufy, and fhews *Shake-*
fpear perfectly underftood the *Jeu du Theatre.*

REMARK LI.

ACT V. SCENE 1

Pro. ———— fay, my Spirit,
How fares the King and's Followers?
Ar. Confin'd
In the fame Fafhion as you gave in Charge;
Juft as you left them, all your Prifoners, Sir,
In the Lime-Grove which Weather fends your Cell.
They cannot budge, till your Releafe. The King,
His Brother, and yours, abide all three diftracted;
And the Remainder, *mourning over them,*
Brim-full of Sorrow, and Difmay : But chiefly,
Him that you term'd the good old Lord *Gonzalo.*
His Tears run down his Beard, like Winter-drops
From Eaves of Reeds : Your Charm fo ftrongly works
            'em,
That if you now beheld them, your Affections
Wou'd become tender.
Pro. Doft thou think fo, Spirit?
Ar. Mine wou'd, Sir, were I human.
Pro. And mine fhall.
Haft thou, which art but Air, a Touch, a Feeling,
Of their Affections, and fhall not my felf,
One of their Kind, (g) that relifh all as fharply,
Paffion as they, be kindlier mov'd than thou art?

(g) *That relifh all as fharply,* &c.] Mr. *Pope*
chang'd *Paffion* here, to *paffion'd,* which Mr. *Theob.*
(*p.* 64. *n.* 28.) explodes, infifting " all the Authen-
tic Copies read

            ——— Paffion *as they,*

                                    which

which is very true: But they, and he after them,
and Mr. *Warb.* (*p.* 74.) after him, ufe it here as a
Verb, on one fingle Authority of the Poet;

   ‘ *Dumbly fhe* paffions, *frantickly fhe doateth.’*
VENUS and ADONIS.

Which, however ferviceable it might prove towards
clearing up, and fupporting any fufpected, or dubious Paffage, is no Way neceffary, or ufeful here,
where the Pointing alone wants to be rectified thus:

——— that relifh all as fharply
Paffion as they, ———

the Poet clearly meaning to make *Profpero* fay, he
relifh'd all Paffion, as fharply, as Alonzo *and the reft*;
or, (if it fhould be thought better) *he relifh'd Paffion all* [full] *as fharply as they*, and no more: The
prefent Pointing and Comments thereon, making
Shakefpear full as guilty, (if not guiltier) of Tautology, as in *bafelefs Fabric*, and *infubftantial Pageant*,
(which Mr. *Warb.* as has been fhewn, is highly dif-
gufted with) (14) to relifh, or feel Paffion, and to
paffion, being nearly fynonymous.

REMARK LII.

SCENE II.

Pro. (h) Ye Elves of Hills, Brooks, ftanding Lakes,
     and Groves;
And ye that on the Sands with printlefs Foot,
Do chafe the ebbing *Neptune,* and do fly him,

(14) Remark XLIX. p. 77.

When

When he comes back; you demy Puppets, that
By Moon-fhine, do the green, four Ringlets make,
Whereof the Ewe not bites; and you, whofe Paftime
Is to make Midnight Mufhrooms, that rejoice
To hear the folemn Curfew: By whofe Aid,
(Weak Mafters tho' ye be) I have bedimm'd
The Noon-tide Sun; call'd forth the mutinous Winds;
And 'twixt the green Sea, and the azur'd Vault,
Set roaring War: To the dread ratling Thunder
Have I given Fire; and rifted *Jove*'s ftout Oak,
With his own Bolt: The ftrong-bas'd Promontory
Have I made fhake; and by the Spurs pluck'd up
The Pine, and Cedar: (i) Graves at my Command,
Have wak'd their Sleepers; op'd, and let them forth,
By my fo potent Art. ———

(h) *Shakefpear*, in this beautiful Incantation, has
fhewn beyond Contradiction, he was perfectly acquainted with the Sentiments of the Ancients, on
the Subject of Enchantments. *Ovid*'s Metamor-
phofes, *Book* vii. from *v.* 197, to *v.* 206. were his
Foundation; but he has varied the Plan with a
mafterly Judgment, having omitted Circumftances,
which, though then fuppofed to be practifed, and
therefore ornamental to the *Roman Poet*, would
have made no Figure (being difufed) in the *Britifh
Bard*; and by the happy Fire of his own Imagination, greatly improv'd thofe he thought fit to take
Notice of; as any Judge may perceive, by compar-
ing the following Verfes from *Ovid*, with the above
Lines of *Shakefpear*.

*Auræque, & venti, montefque, amnefque, lacufque,
Diique omnes nemorum, diique omnes noctis adefte :
Quorum ope, cum volui, ripis mirantibus amnes
In fontes redire fuos : concuffaque fifto,*

Stantia

Stantia concutio cantu freta ; nubila pello,
Nubilaque induco ; ventos abigoque vocoque :
* * * * * * * * * * * *
Et silvas moveo ; Jubeoq; tremiscere montes ;
Et MUGIRE solum, MANESQUE exire SEPULCHRIS.

(i) ——— ———*Graves at my Command,*
Have wak'd their Sleepers ; op'd and let them forth]
Mr. *Warb.* p. 75. *n.* 5. transposes and alters these
Words thus ;

——— *Graves at my Command,*
Have open'd and let forth their Sleepers, wak'd
By my so potent Art.

which he insists is the right Reading, and says the
old Text is guilty of an " *absurd Transposition*," and
is very severe on Mr. *Theob.* who, *p.* 65. *n.* 29. tho'
he thinks the Expression is odd, endeavours to
justify it, from two Authorities nearly analo-
gous.

The first from *Virgil*, who makes *Anchises* say to
Æneas, speaking of *Romulus*,

En hujus, nate, auspiciis illa inclyta Roma,
Imperium terris, animos equabit *Olympo,*
(15) Septemque una sibi muro circumdabit arces.

Lo, Son! beneath th' Influence of his Reign,
Rome *the renown'd*, shall stretch *her wide Domain,*
To the Earth's Bounds ; her Valour to the Skies :
And bid *round seven Hills* her Walls arise.

(15) Mr. *Theob.* only gives this Line, not considering that
EQUABIT, as well as CIRCUMDABIT is govern'd of *Roma.*

Where

Where *Rome* is made to do more than *Prospero*
pretends his Magic can.

The second, from the *Bonduca* of *Beaumont*
and *Fletcher*, who say, Fame

> Wakens the ruin'd Monuments, *and there*
> *Where nothing but* eternal Death, *and* Sleep *is*,
> Informs *again* the dead Bones.

The firft of thefe Authorities Mr. *Warb.* over-
looks, and endeavours, by finking the laft Line
and Half, to turn the fecond againft him, and give
it quite a foreign Meaning : And fays, " Graves
" waking their Sleepers, muft needs be under-
" ftood literally. For *Prospero* would infinuate,
" that dead Men are *actually raifed to Life*, by his
" Art." O fy! Mr. *Warb.* fy! to forget all your
other Reading, as well as your Bible, Sir! To
raife the *Ghofts*, the *Shades* of the Dead,

> ——— *quæ rerum* fimulachra *vocamus*,

has from the Witch of *Endor* downwards, been
fuppofed to be within the Compafs of the Pro-
feffors of Magic, but for them " *to raife the*
" *Dead actually to Life*" is a Power, *poor Shake-*
fpear, nor any other Author but yourfelf, dear
Sir, ever intrufted them with.

And fure, had Mr. *Warb.* confider'd his own
Obfervation on this Paffage being borrow'd from
Ovid, a little more maturely ; and regarded MU-
GIRE SOLUM, as well as *Manefque exire Sepulchris*,
he would poffibly, have fpar'd the Sneer upon his
Brother Critic, and have let the Text of his Au-
thor flept undifturb'd : That Groaning of the
Ground, being a fufficient Caufe for *Shakefpear* to
make

make the *Graves wake their Sleepers* therewith, at
PROSPERO's *Command*, before *they op'd by his so
patent Art to let them forth* ; and 'tis more than probable he chofe fo to do, rather than like Mr. *Warb.*
make them walk in their Sleep.

And indeed it requires fome Skill in *literal Criticifm,* to know which this Gentleman wou'd have
wak'd, the *Graves,* or their *Sleepers* ; fince his
Words require no great Pains to be read, and
underftood in the following Manner:

   —— Graves at my Command
Have wak'd; open'd, and let forth their Sleepers,
By my fo potent Art.

Which will fhew (tho' it may not convince*)* him
that *abfurd Tranfpofitions,* may be charg'd to any
Editor's Account ; as nothing is eafier, than to infift with a very dogmatic Air, that the laft Reading of his Words, is the righteft, and what he
undoubtedly wrote.

REMARK LIII.

———— But this rough Magic
I here abjure : And when I have requir'd
Some heavenly Mufic, (which even now I do*)*
To work mine End upon their Senfes ; (k) that,
This airy Charm *is for :* I'll break my Staff,
(l) Bury it *certain Fathoms* in the Earth ;
And deeper than did ever Plummet found,
I'll drown my Book.

(k) —

(k)———— ———— ————*That*
This airy Charm is for ; ————] This Paſſage
Mr. *Warb. p.* 76. *n.* 6. has alter'd to,

———— *that*
This airy Charm HAS FRAIL'D ;————

and ſays a great deal in ſupport of his Alteration :
But poſſibly, if *this airy Charm* (which *this Editor*
inſiſts, can only refer to the Thunder and Light-
ning, introduc'd in the former Part of the Play)
ſhould be clearly underſtood, to refer to the Invocation of *Elves,* with which *Proſpero* begins this
Speech ; and that the Intent of that Invocation,
was to require and procure, ſome heavenly Muſic,
to break the Charms of his *rough Magic,* which
had caus'd the Tempeſt and Shipwreck ; and
by ſucceeding Terrors, drove them into that
State of melancholy Diſtraction, *Ariel,* but three
Speeches before, told *Proſpero,* (tho' Mr. *Warb.*
forgot it) they were in ; and that, by that Muſic,
he was *to work his End upon,* by reſtoring them to
their Senſes ; for he ſays,

———— *They being Penitent,*

Which was all he propoſed by his rougher Charms ;

The ſole Drift of my Purpoſe doth extend
Not a Frown farther : Go, releaſe them, ARIEL,
My Charms I'll break, their Senſes I'll reſtore,
And they ſhall be themſelves.

And that immediately on *Ariel*'s ſetting about
the Execution of this pleaſing Commiſſion, *Proſ-*
pero invokes all his Spirits ; tells what they have
done,

done, great and terrible, but that he will never ufe them in that Way any more; and then
informs them why he ufes the prefent *airy Charm*,
to require *heavenly Mufic*, and for what Purpofe he
requires it; this Gentleman may fend his auxili-
ary Participle FRAIL'D, a grazing, and admit the
old Reading to he genuine, without any Prejudice
to *Shakefpear*'s good Senfe, or Poetry.

(l) —————————*I'll break my Staff,*
  Bury it certain Fathoms *in the Earth* ;] This
Paffage alfo, has incurr'd the Difpleafure of Mr.
Warb. who (*p. 77. n. 7.*) fays it renders theThought
" *flat and ridiculous*", becaufe *certain*, in its
" prefent Signification is predicated of a precife
" determinate Number." But fure, he did not remember thefe Paffages:

Certain *Ladies or Counteffes.*
HEN. viii. ACT iv. Sc. 2.

fome certain *of the nobleft* Romans.
JUL. CÆS. ACT i. Sc. 6.

—— *I did fend to you,*
For certain *Sums of Gold,* ——
Id. ACT iv. Sc. 3.

—— certain *Players*
We o'er-wrought on the Way, ——
HAM. ACT ii. Sc. 9.

In which Places, 'tis probable, his gteat Sagacity,
would be puzzled to find out *the precife determinate Number,* certain *is predicated* of; and therefore

fore the old Reading may maintain its Poft, notwithftanding his Alteration, to

Bury't a certain *Fadom,* &c.

on the Authority of *Bale* ; who does not contradict
Grammar fo much, as to put the Partitive to a
Noun Singular, when many are to be underftood.

But what is moft furprizing is, that Mr. *Warb.*
who is fo fond of the *French,* from whom we take
the Word, fhould not know, or (which is much
the fame) not remember, that with them, [*Certain*]
in the Plural is equivalent to, and expreffed by
[*quelques uns*] SOME ; which (ufed integrally) never
means a precife determinate Number, unlefs a nu-
meral is join'd with it ; as,

And fome TEN *Voices cried God fave King* Richard.
RICH. iii. ACT iii. Sc. 13.

though it always implies more than One ; and this
his Bible (if he had remembered it) would have
inform'd him ; in which, he may find,

1. *Tunc refponderunt* quidam *e* Scribis *et* Pharifæis.
MATT. xii. 38.

2. *Supervenerint* quidam *Judæi.*   ACTS xiv. 19.

3. *Vero* quidam *ex circulatoribus* Judæis.   *id.* xix. 13.

4. *Sed et* quidam *ex anarchis quum effent ei Amici.*
ibid. 31.

5. Quidam *autem ex* Epicureis, & Stoicis *Philofophis,*
conflictabantur cum eo ; & quidam *dicebant,*
Alor:

Alors quelques uns *d'entre les Philosophes* Epicuriens, *&*
Stoiciens, *s'addresserent en paroles* : *&* les uns *disoient*.
ACTS xvii. 18.

Where *quidam*, which the *French* tranflate *quelques
uns*, is by us rendered *certain*.

1. *Then* certain *of the* Scribes *and* Pharifees *answered*.

2. *And there came thither* certain *Jews*.

3. *And* certain *vagabond* Jews.

4. *And* certain *of the chief of* Afia *that were his Friends*.

5. *Then* certain *of the Philofophers of the* Epicureans,
and of the Stoics, *encountred him*, and fome *said*.

as likewife, that his Favourite A CERTAIN, is always predicated precifely of one fingle Thing or
Perfon, and never ufed indefinitely : as,

Quidam *Scriba* —— a certain *Scribe*. MATT. viii. 19.

Ecce quidam *præfectus venit* —— *behold their came* a certain *Ruler*. *id.* ix. 18.

Adiit eum quidam. —— *there came to him* a certain *Man*.
id. xvii. 14

Befides many other Paffages, which if this Gentle
man could fpare Time from his critical Studies to
perufe, would abundantly fatisfy him, as it can't
be

be fuppofed he would deny the Authority of the
BOOK.

REMARK LIV.

——— The Charm diffolves apace,
And as the Morning fteals upon the Night,
Melting the Darknefs ; fo their rifing Senfes,
Begin to chafe the (m) *ignorant Fumes*, that mantle
Their clearer Reafon.

(m) *Begin to chafe the* ignorant Fumes] Mr. *Warb.*
(*p.* 73. *) comments on *ignorant Fumes*, and fays,
ignorant here means hurtful to Reafon, how far the
Editor fpeaks from Experience he fays not ; but
the Poet meant no more, than is convey'd by the
plain Senfe of the Words ; making them at the
Sound of " *a folemn Air* " finely call'd

——————— the beft Comforter
To an unfettled Fancy———

begin to fhake off that Weight of Horror, that
ftupifying Terror they had labour'd under, which
had covered their Senfes like a Cloud, wrapt up
their Underftandings as in a Mantle, and made
their Brains, *ufelefs, boil within their Sculls!* and,
as this laft Airy-Charm work'd, the other diffolv'd,
till by Degrees they were perfectly reftored. And
this Reftoration, he has beautifully illuftrated with
the above metaphorical Simile, plainly defcribing
the *Effects*, but not at all declaring the *Qualities* of
Ig-

IGNORANCE, leaving that to be done by her more
intimate Acquaintance.

R E M A R K LV.

A R I E L *sings.*

(n) *Where the Bee sucks, there* suck *I* ;
In a Cowslip Bell I lie :
There I couch when Owls do cry ;
On the Bat's Back I do fly
(o) *After* Summer : *Merrily,*
Merrily, merrily shall I live now,
Under the Blossom that hangs on the Bough.

(n) *Where the Bee* sucks, *&c.*] Here the Reve-
rend Editor's Ill-nature gives Place to his Wit,
and having sufficiently reprov'd, he now laughs
at his Brother *Theob.* who, *p. 66. n. 31.* has changed
suck for *lurk* ; but we owe his good Humour
to the Pleasantness of the Subject, [*sucking*]
which calls to his Mind the Idea of being
" brought up to good Eating and Drinking,"
(*p. 78. n. 8.*) Employments he seems to hold
in some tolerable Degree of Esteem, not to say
Fondness, if any Judgment may be form'd from
the frequent Opportunities taken to mention and
pay some Marks of his Regard to them : As in
a Scene or two before this, he has taken great
Care to point out *Stephano*'s and *Trinculo*'s La-
mentations for the Loss of their Bottle, as a particular Beauty ; and a few Scenes after this, has
given us a long Note, to prove he holds *Sack* to be
the only real *Elixir.*

(o) *After*

(o) *After Summer merrily,*] As Mr. *Warb.* in this
p. 79. *n.* 9. and the laſt cited Paſſage, ſupports the
old Reading, (Mr. *Theob.* here, *p.* 66, *n.* 32. altering *Summer* to *Sunſet*) we agree in Opinion : But
the above Pointing is ſubmitted to the Publick,
inſtead of that which has hitherto obtained in all
the Editions, *viz.*

> On the Bat's Back I do fly,
> After Summer merrily.

Except the more modern ones place a Comma after
Summer. This Pointing, if received, may poſſibly put an End to the Diſpute betwixt Summer and Sun-ſet.

REMARK LVI.

Alon. If thou be'ſt *Proſpero,*
Give us Particulars of thy Preſervation ;
How thou haſt met us here, who three Hours ſince
Were wreck'd upon this Shore ? where I have loſt,
(How ſharp the Point of this Remembrance is !)
My dear Son *Ferdinand.*
  Proſ. I am Woe for it, Sir.
  Alon. Irreparable is the Loſs, and Patience
Says, it is paſt her Cure.
  Proſ. I rather think,
You have not ſought her Help, of whoſe ſoft Grace,
For the like Loſs, I have her ſovereign Aid,
And reſt my ſelf content.
  Alon. You the like Loſs !
  Proſ. As great to me, as late ; and ſupportable
To make the dear Loſs, have I Means much weaker
                                        Than

Than you may call to comfort you : For I
Have loft my Daughter.

   Alon. A Daughter ? (p)
O Heav'ns ! that they were living both in *Naples,*
The King and Queen there ; that they were, I wifh,
My felf mudded in that oozey Bed
Where my Son lies.

(p) *A Daughter?*] This beautiful Preparative to
the principal Difcovery, and artful Manner of
obtaining *Alonfo*'s Confent to the Marriage of
his Son with *Miranda,* is an Incident as happily
managed as any in the whole Play ; and fhews
Shakefpear's Knowledge of the Stage, to be e-
qual to, and govern'd by, that he had of Nature.

R E M A R K LVII.

Miranda *and* Ferdinand *difcovered playing at Chefs.*

   Mir. Sweet Lord, you play me falfe.
   Ferd. No, my dear Love,
I wou'd not for the World.
   Mir. (q) Yes, *for a Score of Kingdoms,* you fhou'd
     wrangle,
And I wou'd call it fair Play.

(q) Yes, *for a Score of Kingdoms,* &c.] Mr.
Warb. p. 82. *n.* 1. very gravely gives an Explanation of this Paffage, faying, it means " if the
" *Subject* or *Bet* were Kingdoms: *Score* here not
" fignifying the Number Twenty but Account."
                  But

But if this great Man had made any Account of *Shakespear*'s Senfe, he might have feen evidently, the Poet here meant neither more nor lefs than the Number Twenty ; putting that fmall Portion of the World in Oppofition to the Whole, which *Ferdinand* had juft mentiond ; and probably had in Mind thofe early Times, when there was a much larger Number of Kingdoms, or Governments in *Italy* it felf, than are here mentioned.

And if this accurate Critic had exerted his ufual Sharpnefs, he would poffibly have found we fhou'd read *wrong me* for *wrangle* ; (16) " to preferve the " Sentiment :" Fraud, the Caufe being mention'd, when fhe faid he play'd her *falfe*, and not *wrangling* the Effect, tho' 'tis not unufual with *Shakefpear* to fubftitute the one for the other.

REMARK LVIII.

Alon. Is not this *Stephano* my drunken Butler ?

Seb. He is drunk now ; where had he Wine ?

Alon. And *Trinculo* is reeling ripe : (r) Where fhou'd they

Find this *grand Liquor* that has gilded them ?

How cam'ft thou in this Pickle ?

Trin. I have been in fuch a *Pickle*, fince I faw you laft, I fear me will never *out of my Bones :* I fhall not fear Fly-blowing.

Seb. Why how now, *Stephano ?*

Ste. (s) O touch me not : I am not *Stephano*, but a Cramp.

(16) A Reafon frequently affigned by Meffrs. *Theob.* and *Warb.* in fupport of their Alterations, Tranfpofitions, and Interpolations.

(r) —

(r) —————— *where fhou'd they*
Find this grand Liquor *that has gilded them ?*]
That *Shakefpear* here alluded to the cant Name
of the Chemifts, for their pretended univerfally
Reftorative, and generative Liquor, ELIXIR, then
fo much in Vogue, is undoubted ; but for all that,
and Mr. *Warb.* " to be fure, *Shakefpear* wrote ——
" *grand* 'LIXIR." *p.* 86, *n.* 4. the old Reading may
maintain its Poft againft all his Authorities ; ne'er
a one of which prove any Thing more, than that
other Poets adopted the Term, and ufed it, and
its pretended Effects metaphorically : But indeed,
are a Sort of Proof this Gentleman is no Enemy
to Sack ; tho' he does not inform us, whether he
knows the Sack fo often mentioned by the Poets
of thofe Times, was chiefly, if not only, Sherry.

(s) *O touch me not, I am not* Stephano, *but a*
Cramp.] Mr. *Warb.* (p. 87. *n.* 5.) tells us his Sup-
pofition, that an *Italian* Quibble lurk'd under thefe
Words, which he apprehends in the Original were,
Io non fono Stephano *mai* Staffilato ; and *Staffilato,*
he fays, fignifies a Man well lafh'd, or flead ; but
if he had recollected *Trinculo*'s Anfwer, (and they
were both pretty much in the fame Condition) he
wou'd have found the Pain complain'd of, went
farther than *Skin-deep*, for he fears 'twill never out
of his *Bones* ; and a Man might very *ferioufly* fear
being handled in fuch a Condition, as plain as
Mr. *Warb.* finds a *Joke* was intended : But, as *Ham-*
let fays,

—— *Let the* gall'd Jade *winch, our Withers are unwrung.*

F I N I S.

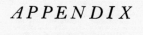

APPENDIX

REMARKS

ON THE

TEMPEST.

[Price One Shilling and Six-Pence.]

Shortly will be Printed,

PROPOSALS

For Publiſhing by SUBSCRIPTION,

SHAKESPEAR's PLAYS,

FREED

From the *literary* and *punctuary* Errors of the
EARLIEST IMPRESSIONS ;

AND

RESCUED from the many *falſe Emendations*, and
forced Interpretations,

Of the LATER EDITIONS.

To which will be added,

The Hiſtory, Plot, Diſpoſition, and Chronology
(ſo far as it can be ſettled) of each Play ; with
the Alluſions to, and Imitations or Reſemblances
of, the Ancients, as they ſeverally occur :

WITH

The various Readings, of all the Editions now
extant, ſubjoined.

N. B. Whoever is inclined to encourage this
Undertaking, may, by applying to Meſſrs.
Manby and *Cox*, on *Ludgate-Hill*, be informed
of the Conditions.

REMARKS

ON THE

TEMPEST:

OR AN

ATTEMPT

To Rescue

SHAKESPEAR

FROM THE

Many Errors falfely charged on him, by his
feveral Editors.

To which is prefixed,

A fhort Account of the Story, Plot, Difpofition
and Chronology, of the Play;

AS

A Plan, for a new Edition of that Author.

by — Holt.

The Ambition of one Sort *of* SCHOLARS *is to increafe the Num-*
ber of various Lections; *which they have done to fuch a Degree*
of obfcure Diligence, *that we now begin to value the* firft Editions *of* Books, *as moft* CORRECT, *becaufe they have been* leaft
CORRECTED.   POPE's *Obf. on* HOMER, P. 1.

LONDON:
Printed for the AUTHOR,
And Sold by Meffieurs MANBY and COX, on *Ludgate-Hill.*
MDCCL.

PUBLISHER'S ADVERTISEMENT

EIGHTEENTH CENTURY SHAKESPEARE

During the one hundred and seven years covered by this series, the reputation of William Shakespeare as poet and dramatist rose from a controversial and highly qualified acceptance by post-Restoration critics and "improvers" to the almost idolatrous admiration of the early Romantics and their immediate precursors. Imposing its own standards and interpretations upon Shakespeare, the Eighteenth Century scrutinized his work in various lights. Certain qualities of the plays were isolated and discussed by a parade of learned, cantankerous, and above all self-assured commentators.

Thirty-five of the most important and representative books and pamphlets are here presented in twenty-six volumes; many of the works, through the very fact of their limited circulation have become extremely scarce, and when obtainable, expensive and fragile. The series will be useful not only for the student of Shakespeare's reputation in the period, but for all those interested in eighteenth century taste, taste-making, scholarship, and theatre. Within the series we may follow the arguments and counter-arguments as they appeared to contemporary playgoers and readers, and the shifting critical emphases characteristic of the whole era.

In an effort to provide responsible texts of these works, strict editorial principles have been established and followed. All relevant editions have been compared, the best selected, and the reasons for the choice given. Furthermore, at least one other copy, frequently three or more, have been collated with the copy actually reproduced, and the collations recorded. In cases where variants or cancels exist, every attempt has been made to provide both earlier and later or indifferently varying texts, as appendices. Each volume is preceded by a short preface discussing the text, the publication history, and, when necessary, critical and biographical considerations not readily available.

1. 1692   **Thomas Rymer**
           A Short View of Tragedy (1693)
           xvi, 184p.

2. 1693   **John Dennis**
           The Impartial Critick: or, some observations upon a late
           book, entitled, A Short View of Tragedy, written by
           Mr. Rymer, and dedicated to the Right Honourable Charles
           Earl of Dorset, etc. (1693)
           xvi, 52p.
    1712   **John Dennis**
           An Essay on the Genius and Writings of Shakespear: with
           some Letters of Criticism to the Spectator (1712)
           xxii, 68p.

3. 1694   **Charles Gildon [ed.]**
           Miscellaneous Letters and Essays, on Several Subjects. Philo-
           sophical, Moral, Historical, Critical, Amorous, etc. in Prose
           and Verse (1694)
           xvi, 132p.

4. 1710   **Charles Gildon**
           The Life of Mr. Thomas Betterton, the late Eminent Trage-
           dian. Wherein The Action and Utterance of the Stage, Bar,
           and Pulpit, are distinctly consider'd . . . To which is added,
           The Amorous Widow, or the Wanton Wife . . . Written by
           Mr. Betterton. Now first printed from the Original Copy
           (1710)
           xvi, 176, 87p.

5. 1726   **Lewis Theobald**
           Shakespeare restored: or, A Specimen of the Many Errors,
           As well Committed, as Unamended, by Mr. Pope in his Late
           Edition of this Poet (1726)
           xiii, 194p. 4°

6. 1747   **William Guthrie**
           An Essay upon English Tragedy with Remarks upon the
           Abbe de Blanc's Observations on the English Stage (?1747)
           34p.
    1749   **John Holt**
           An Attempte to Rescue that Aunciente, English Poet, and

Play-wrighte, Maister Williaume Shakespere, from the Maney Errours, faulsely charged on him, by Certaine New-fangled Wittes and to let him speak for Himself, as right well he wotteth, when Freede from the many Careless Mistakeings, of the Heedless first Imprinters, of his Workes (1749)
94p.

7. **1748** **Thomas Edwards**
The Canons of Criticism and Glossary. Being a Supplement to Mr. Warburton's Edition of Shakespear. Collected from the Notes in that celebrated Work, and proper to be bound up with it. To which are added, The Trial of the Letter Υ alias Y; and Sonnets (Seventh Edition, with Additions 1765) 368p.

8. **1748** **Peter Whalley**
An Enquiry into the Learning of Shakespeare (1748)
84p.
   1767 **Richard Farmer**
As Essay on the Learning of Shakespeare ... the Second Edition, with Large Additions (1767)
viii, 96p.

9. **1752** **William Dodd**
The Beauties of Shakespeare: Regularly selected from each Play, With a General Index, Digesting them under Proper Heads. Illustrated with Explanatory Notes and Similar Passages from Ancient and Modern Authors (1752)
2v., xxiv, 264; iv, 258p.

10. **1753** **Charlotte Ramsay Lennox**
Shakespear Illustrated ... with Critical Remarks (1753-4)
3v., xiv, 292; iv, 276; iv, 312p.

11. **1765** **William Kenrick**
A Review of Doctor Johnson's New Edition of Shakespeare: In which the Ignorance, or Inattention of That Editor is exposed, and the Poet Defended from the Persecution of his Commentators (1765)
xvi, 136p.
   1766 **Thomas Tyrwhitt**
Observations and Conjectures upon some Passages of

Shakespeare (1766)
ii, 56p.

12. 1769   **Elizabeth Montagu**
An Essay on the Writings and Genius of Shakespear, compared with the Greek and French dramatic Poets. With some
remarks upon the misrepresentations of Mons. de Voltaire
(1769)
iv, 288p.

13. 1774   **William Richardson**
    1784   Essays on Shakespeare's Dramatic Characters: With an
    1789   Illustration of Shakespeare's Representation of National
           Character, in that of Fluellen (sixth edition 1812)
           xii, 448p.

14. 1775   **Elizabeth Griffith**
The Morality of Shakespeare's Drama Illustrated (1775)
xvi, 528p.

15. 1777   **Maurice Morgann**
An Essay on the Dramatic Character of Sir John Falstaff
(1777)
xii, 186p.

16. 1783   **Joseph Ritson**
Remarks Critical and Illustrative of the last Edition of
Shakespeare [by George Steevens, 1778], (1783)
viii, 240p.

    1788   **Joseph Ritson**
The Quip Modest; A few Words by way of Supplement to
Remarks, Critical and Illustrative on the Text and Notes of
the Last Edition of Shakespeare: occasioned by a Republi-
cation of that Edition (1788, first issue)
viii, 32p.
With the preface (revised) to the second issue of *The Quip
Modest* (1788)
viii p.

17. 1785   **Thomas Whately**
Remarks on some of the Characters of Shakespere, Edited

by Richard Whately (Third edition 1839)
128p.

18. 1785   **John Monck Mason**
    1797   Comments on the Several Editions of Shakespeare's Plays,
    1798   Extended to those of Malone and Steevens (1807)
           xvi, 608p.

19. 1786   **John Philip Kemble**
           Macbeth and King Richard the Third: An Essay, in answer to
           Remarks on some of the Characters of Shakespeare [by
           Thomas Whately] (1817)
           xii, 172p.

20. 1792   **Joseph Ritson**
           Cursory Criticisms on the Edition of Shakespeare published
           by Edmond Malone (1792)
           x, 104p.
           Edmond Malone
           A Letter to the Rev. Richard Farmer, D.D. Master of
           Emanuel College, Cambridge; Relative to the Edition of
           Shakespeare, published in 1790. And Some Late Criticisms
           on that work (1792)
           ii, 40p.

21. 1796   **William Henry Ireland**
           An Authentic Account of the Shakespeare Manuscripts (1796)
           ii, 44p.
    1799   **William Henry Ireland**
           Vortigern, An Historical Tragedy, In five Acts; Represented
           at the Theatre Royal, Drury Lane. And Henry the Second,
           An Historical Drama. Supposed to be written by the Author
           of Vortigern (1799)
           80, iv, 79p.

22. 1796   **Edmond Malone**
           An Inquiry into the Authenticity of Certain Miscellaneous
           Papers and Legal Instruments, published Dec. 24, 1795. And
           Attributed to Shakespeare, Queen Elizabeth, and Henry
           Earl of Southampton (1796)
           vii, 424p.

23. 1796 **Thomas Caldecott**
Mr. Ireland's Vindication of his Conduct, Respecting the
Publication of the Supposed Shakespeare Manuscripts (1796)
iv, 48p.

1800 **George Hardinge**
Chalmeriana: or a Collection of Papers ... occasioned by
reading a late Apology for the Believers in the Shakespeare
papers, by George Chalmers etc. (1800)
viii, 94p.

24. 1798 **Samuel Ireland**
An Investigation of Mr. Malone's Claim to the Character of
Scholar, or Critic, Being an Examination of his Inquiry into
the Authenticity of the Shakespeare Manuscripts, etc. (1797)
vi, 156p.

25. 1797 **George Chalmers**
An Apology for the Believers in the Shakespeare-Papers
which were exhibited in Norfolk Street (1797)
iv, 628p.

26. 1799 **George Chalmers**
A Supplemental Apology for the Believers in the Shakespeare-
Papers: Being a Reply to Mr. Malone's Answer, which was
early announced, but never published: with a Dedication to
George Steevens, and a Postscript (1799)
viii, 656 p.